CHILDREN WITH SPECIAL ABILITIES IN THE EARLY YEARS

A Guide For Educators Of Children Aged 3–8

Jo Counsell

CHILDREN WITH SPECIAL ABILITIES IN THE EARLY YEARS

A Guide For Educators Of Children Aged 3–8

Jo Counsell

A division of MA Education Ltd

Teach Books Division, MA Education Ltd, St Jude's Church,
Dulwich Road, London SE24 0PB

British Library Cataloguing-in-Publication Data
A catalogue record is available for this book

ISBN-10: 1 85642 350 6   ISBN-13: 978 1 85642 350 2

Printed by CLE, St Ives, Huntingdon, Cambridgeshire

CONTENTS

BIOGRAPHY

Jo taught Modern Languages at several comprehensive schools before joining the National Association for Gifted Children in 1999 as Education Consultant. She has advised parents, delivered INSET on Gifted and Talented, researched various issues for the DfES and written articles for a number of publications. In 2004 she took up the post of Gifted and Talented Strand Co-ordinator for Hastings and St. Leonards Excellence Cluster, where she works with primary and secondary schools to improve gifted and talented provision throughout the Cluster. She also plays an active role in the regional South East partnership SEAGUL. Her particular interests include motivating and supporting underachieving able students, handwriting difficulties, transition between key stages and schools, home-school liaison and the early years. Jo is married, has four children and lives in Hastings. She can be contacted on jo@hstlexc.net

ACKNOWLEDGEMENTS

There are many people without whose help and patience it would have been impossible to write this book. Perhaps the biggest thanks should go to the National Association for Gifted Children, where I had rich opportunities to learn from experts and encountered many wonderful families. My NAGC colleagues Ken Bore, Gail Devlin-Jones and Lori Ferguson were particularly encouraging of my writing endeavours. My colleagues Jennifer Seaton, Ian Fuller and Carole Dixon at the Hastings and St. Leonards Excellence Cluster continue to provide huge support and inspiration. My parents, Margot and Harry Green, gave me peace and a place to write, and my loving and supportive family – Andi, Pete, Jack, Rebecca and most especially Mike – just about managed to put up with me during the process.

NOTE ABOUT CASE STUDIES

All case studies are based on real children, but in order to protect their anonymity their names have been changed.

INTRODUCTION

The early experiences of educational settings are very important for all children. It is in these early years that they learn whether they like school, whether it has valuable things to offer them, whether they fit in and whether they are succeeding or failing. These early impressions are enormously significant for all that follows, and can be surprisingly difficult to alter later on, when their impact on everyday school life becomes more evident.

It is now generally acknowledged that early intervention for children with many types of special need is immensely valuable. It is also becoming more widely accepted that children with special abilities can benefit from early recognition and intervention, and that offering the appropriate educational environment and provision from an early age can help children to develop their abilities, and educators to recognise them.

More weight is given to the argument for the early nurturing of abilities and talents by recent developments in brain research, which put forward the idea that a significant proportion of total brain development happens before the age of 5, or even earlier (for example, Dryden and Voss 1999, Harrison 2004). The early years are viewed by experts in brain development as an optimum stage for many kinds of learning, for example, a foreign language, at a time when the drive to communicate and develop language is at its peak.

The rationale for writing this book about children in the early years comes from my own experience working on the helpline for the National Association for Gifted Children (NAGC – see 'Useful Websites' at the back of this book for contact details), where most of the calls relate to children between the ages of three and eight, and the peak ages are four to five. Clearly this is an age group in which problems are encountered by many parents as well as schools and nurseries, and so it is important to address the needs of very young children at an age when it is still possible to make a real and lasting difference.

Jo Counsell, 2007

CHAPTER 1

DEFINITIONS OF HIGH ABILITY AND GIFTEDNESS

WHY 'CHILDREN WITH SPECIAL ABILITIES'?

Any discussion of high ability issues is fraught with controversy, not least over what particular terminology to use. The word 'gifted' has been widely used in different parts of the world over many years, particularly in the US and increasingly in Britain with the advent of the 'Gifted and Talented' initiatives from about 1998. It is used in many of the journals and much of the literature that relates to high ability, and so will be used here when discussing relevant texts and theories. It can be a problematic term, however, for a number of reasons.

The first difficulty is that the word 'gifted' implies a simple separation – either a person is gifted or they are not. Many who research and work in the field of high ability do not view the reality in this way, but as much more complex with many individual variations. Some may prefer to think in terms of a continuum (for example: able, highly able, exceptionally able) and to relate this to different types of ability (for example a more able mathematician).

A second, related, problem is that the term 'Gifted and Talented' can give the impression that fixed ability has been bestowed on a person, regardless of any participation in the matter. Again, this does not accord with the way many experts and educators view the development of children who have high abilities or potential, as whatever natural abilities they may have also need recognising and nurturing if they are to develop.

Furthermore, the word 'gifted' is often used globally rather than specifically, implying that a person is highly able at everything, which is unlikely to be the case. Often it is used to mean 'of a high general intelligence', but this does not allow for individual differences and the multiple aspects of intelligence, concepts that are valued by many. Its use may be considered less problematic in more specific phrases such as 'a gifted footballer'.

There is also the difficulty of the connotations which may be associated with the word 'gifted', which often cause problems for both parents and teachers. For many people the implications are of rare or exceptional ability, perhaps bordering on genius. It is often considered an elite term, perhaps because of some of the objections raised above, and therefore does not fit comfortably with the inclusive principles enshrined by our education system. It cannot easily be used in educational contexts without further definition, and this can vary significantly.

In this book, for all of these reasons, it has been decided to use the term 'children with special abilities' as a global term (this terminology is current in New Zealand, see for example Taylor 2002). This reflects and connects with the widespread use of the term 'children with special needs', and labels the ability rather than the child. However, the book will contain many other terms too, as these are widely used by practitioners, researchers, writers, advisers and others with whom educators will come into contact.

WHAT IS MEANT BY 'SPECIAL ABILITIES'?

There have been many debates, especially in the last hundred years or so, about what constitutes high ability, and about the nature of intelligence and whether it can be measured. It is not the purpose of this book to provide an exhaustive examination of all the theories, or to present them in depth. References are provided so that the interested reader can research further. An excellent overview of many differing theories of intelligence and giftedness relating to young children, including models of how highly able potential can be realised, is provided in Porter (1999). For those who wish to delve deeper, the arguments outlined in Sternberg and Davidson (1986) are still highly relevant and interesting. A few of the more influential models and theories have been selected for inclusion here, followed in the next chapter by important theories of child development which seem highly relevant to any discussion of children's growing competences and abilities.

INTELLIGENCE QUOTIENT (IQ)

The notion of IQ has been around for over a hundred years. One example of early psychometric research on the measurement of intelligence can be seen in the work of Binet in France. With his colleague, Simon, he devised a series of age-graded tasks, refined through experimentation. He thus originated the concept of 'mental age', but he rejected the view of intelligence as hereditary and fixed at birth. He saw it rather as multifaceted and complex, capable of being nurtured and increased (see for example Bergin and Cizek, 2001 and Crocker, 1999). Binet's ideas were taken up by Terman, a researcher at Stanford University, who revised and developed the tests on samples of Californian children. These revisions became the 'Stanford-Binet' intelligence test, the updated version of which is still in use in some parts of the world today. The 'Intelligence Quotient' was arrived at by taking the mental age, dividing by the chronological age and then multiplying by 100 to eliminate decimals. (This method of arriving at an IQ score is no longer used, modern scores being based on standard deviations from the norm). Early uses of intelligence tests included the mass testing of recruits to the American military during the first World War in order to deploy them more efficiently, but they were soon put to more questionable uses, for example to screen immigrants arriving in America. As some parts of the tests relied on knowledge of cultural norms and values, the results of the tests were taken by some to lend weight to theories of innate differences in the intelligence of racial groups. Later versions of IQ tests were developed more carefully to take into account different cultural experiences, although they cannot be said to be completely culture-free as they still depend heavily on shared understanding of language.

The IQ test that is now most widely used in the United Kingdom was developed by Wechsler. Currently, children aged 3-5 can be tested on the WPPSI-R (Wechsler Preschool and Primary – Revised Edition) and those aged 6 or above on WISC – III (Wechsler Intelligence Scale for Children – 3rd Edition). A fourth edition has been produced, but at the time of going to press is not yet widely available. Apart from any arguments about the reliability or validity of the tests, there can be a practical issue for very young children. To complete all the sub-tests necessary for assessment takes a considerable amount of time, which may be impossible for a young child to manage efficiently in one session. If the test is being carried out privately, as is often the case with a highly able child, it cannot be spread over several sessions and the score may therefore represent an underperformance. As with all types of test, factors such as good nutrition and a comfortable testing environment free of distractions can affect the score as well.

IQ scores are norm-referenced; that is, they provide a comparison with the average performance for children of the same age. The average score on an IQ test is always 100. On the Wechsler scales, a score of 130 or more (two standard deviations above the mean) has traditionally been considered to be indicative of intellectual giftedness. This represents a performance within the top 2.5 percent (approximately) of the population across a range of sub-tests. Certainly a child achieving such a score (which for the reasons given above may still be an under-performance) can be considered to have a high degree of academic potential, and it is important to take this seriously, especially if the potential has not been identified in other ways.

Critics of IQ tests point out, however, that the tests do not measure non-academic abilities, and that they can give the impression that ability is a single entity which is fixed in a particular individual. It has been noted above that external factors can affect IQ performance, and an improvement in circumstances (eg. better nutrition or a more enriched home or educational environment) could therefore lead to an increased performance. There have even been experiments which have appeared to show that listening to certain kinds of music or taking vitamin supplements can enhance test performance, at least in the short term (for example see Rauscher *et al* 1993 and Schoenthaler *et al* 1991). If environmental factors are important in the development of intelligence, then it follows that it is crucial for appropriate provision to be made in educational settings, as many young children spend a considerable amount of time in them.

IQ tests certainly have their limitations and cannot tell us everything we need to know about any particular child, but the information they provide can be valuable as part of the picture. They can identify highly able children who are under-achieving in school. These children may have emotional or behavioural issues which are disguising unmet ability needs, or they may have learning difficulties or motor skill problems which make school work difficult.

MULTIPLE INTELLIGENCE THEORY

Central to the concept of IQ testing is that there is such a thing as 'general intelligence' (sometimes called g). This notion has been increasingly challenged in recent years, most influentially by Howard Gardner (1983) in his multiple intelligence theory.

He originally described seven different intelligences:

- logical-mathematical
- linguistic
- spatial
- musical
- bodily-kinaesthetic
- interpersonal
- intrapersonal

These are seen initially by Gardner as 'biological potentials', and given the right encouragement and framework can develop into full-blown gifts and talents. Gardner argues that most people will develop some measure of competence in each of the different intelligences, but the potential for development may be much stronger in one or two than in the others. However, the eventual outcome will depend on opportunities and experiences as well as on the natural aptitude (for example, a musically intelligent child needs an outlet for that talent, and encouragement from others, in order to develop it).

Since formulating his original list, Gardner has suggested adding an eighth intelligence, naturalist, to the original list. The possibility of an existential or spiritual intelligence has also been suggested. The list can never be definitive, as this is not intended to be an exact representation of fact, but it is a useful model.

Multiple intelligence theory has been enormously influential in educational thought and practice. Highlighting forms of intelligence which, at least within the western educational context, have previously been undervalued (for example spatial), and embracing social and personal aspects of intelligence have been welcomed as positive contributions to the discussion of high ability within an inclusive framework (for example see Hymer and Michel, 2002 and Smith, 1998).

THREE-RING CONCEPTION OF GIFTEDNESS

Renzulli (1986) sees giftedness as an interaction between three factors: above average ability, task commitment and creativity (*Figure 1*).

For Renzulli, high ability is only one component of what he calls 'creative-productive accomplishment'. It is clear from this that the model he is putting forward is more about how to turn potential into successful achievement, rather than a definition of intelligence as such. His research, writing and practice relating to the provision of suitable educational opportunities for the development and recognition of talents and gifts have been considerably influential, and will be referred to again later in this book.

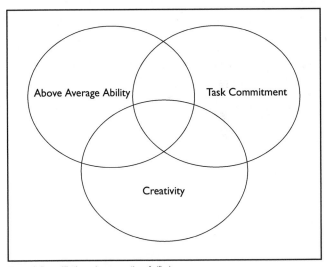

Figure 1: Renzulli's three-ring conception of giftedness

Sternberg (1997) puts forward three types of ability in his triarchic model: **analytic** skills, **synthetic** skills and **practical** problem-solving. He argues that the ability to use these three skills appropriately constitutes an important part of the definition of giftedness.

There are many other important models and theories that could have been included here, perhaps most notably Gagné's model which has been very influential. This is a more complex model and the interested reader will find more information on the web, or in Porter (1999). From the concepts presented above, it can be seen that there is no one agreed way to define high ability, or children with special abilities or talents. There have been many attempts to put forward definitions in recent years, as government policy has sought to find effective ways to provide for more able children in schools (see for example the DfES and QCA websites in the '*Useful Websites*' section at the back of this book).

It is not the purpose of this book to provide a tight definition of high ability or to seek to limit its manifestation to any arbitrary figure (whether an IQ score or a percentage of children). Rather, the attempt is to help teachers and other practitioners recognise and nurture all kinds of abilities, and to highlight the importance of dealing with these in the context of the children's families and culture, as well as school.

CHAPTER 2

LEARNING AND TEACHING IN CONTEXT

All educational practice implies a theoretical stance on the educator's part.

Paulo Freire, 1972.

The history of educational thought and practice is a long and complicated one. It is therefore not possible to do justice in this book to the rich heritage of philosophy and theory from which much of our modern educational system derives. This chapter attempts to look at some of the more influential thinkers and pioneers who have shaped early education in particular, and to draw out the ideas which seem to be the most relevant in providing a theoretical grounding for the discussion of the education of children with special abilities in the early years. Key texts and references are provided for those who wish to pursue their interest further.

FROEBEL

The idea that educational experiences for young children should be provided in a qualitatively different way from those for older pupils can be traced perhaps most strongly back to Froebel in the early part of the nineteenth century. He invented the term 'kindergarten', which became so popular in many parts of the world. He in turn was influenced heavily by the ideas of Rousseau and Pestalozzi, particularly with regard to the importance of the natural environment and the individual freedom of children to learn by interaction with their surroundings. He proposed a model of play-based learning for children up to the age of about eight years old. This has had a major impact on early education through much of Europe and North America, advocating a carefully facilitated and organised provision involving physical objects, songs and games. He saw play as 'an educational medium for understanding the external world' (Walsh *et al*, 2001). He also coined the phrase 'child-centred', which has continued to resonate with early years educators to the present day.

JOHN DEWEY

Dewey's work and legacy have had a profound impact on North American and European schooling, and his status as a philosopher with a genuine and pragmatic interest in education continues to be revered by many. His interest was in pedagogy. He eschewed any absolute doctrine in favour of a more experimental approach which embraced many principles thought by some to be in opposition, such as theory and practice or vocational and academic learning. These dualisms, which he abhorred, still resonate with educational thinkers and practitioners today, and Dewey's beliefs seem as relevant to our schools now as they did in the late nineteenth century. Perhaps most relevant to this discussion is the importance he placed on the teacher's role 'in helping to link children's interests to sustained intellectual development' (Apple and Teitelbaum, 2001).

MARIA MONTESSORI

In 1896 Maria Montessori became the first woman to graduate from medical school in Italy. Her attention soon turned to education, where her work with disadvantaged children and the system of education she developed soon drew attention from around the world. Her impact continues today; there are Montessori nurseries and early learning centres all over the UK and in many other parts of the world. Many teachers are trained in the 'Montessori Method' and this continues to spread the influence of her ideas.

In her writings, Montessori laid out in great detail her teaching methods for young children when introducing them to concepts such as mathematics and language. To back up the methods there are many prescribed materials (such as rods of different length in arithmetic), some of which (or their derivatives) are now in common use in early years settings. While her methods may seem unduly doctrinaire to some, the beliefs behind them are important and are echoed by much current early years practice. One of these principles, applied to all curriculum areas, is the importance of touch and direct experience (for example sandpaper letters for a multi-sensory approach to writing). This is also linked to the natural curiosity of the child which dictates the pace of learning. An important principle for children with particular abilities is that artificial limits are not set for the young child, with some of the apparatus in mathematics representing numbers up to a thousand (see *Chapter 8* for an example of this).

JEAN PIAGET

Piaget lived throughout his life in Switzerland. He received a succession of academic posts and honours, and created a prodigious output of books and papers. Much of his research and observation centred round the development of the child as a self-directed learner, and on how children's natural creativity could be fostered and enhanced by educational experiences.

Piaget's influence on theories of child development and on educational practice has been considerable, and for many trainee teachers and early educators he is primarily remembered for his 'ages and stages' theory, identifying four stages of cognitive development through which children pass. He was a passionate advocate of the child as an autonomous learner, discovering and making sense of the world. These theories were included in the 1967 Plowden Report and incorporated into many British classrooms, but lack of flexibility in the way they were applied and the frequent misapplication of the basic principles led to the discrediting of Piaget's ideas, at least for some educators. However, his influence can still be seen in early learning settings in the continued and increasing emphasis on discovery-based learning. For early educators who are concerned with recognising and nurturing ability, the Piagetian view of children as active agents in their learning who need the right kind of stimulation in order for this to happen effectively is a persuasive one. Schaffer in his study of social development summarises Piaget's importance as follows:

> *It is thus not surprising that Piagetian ideas have had a considerable influence on educational theory; the interplay of maturational readiness and challenging experience forms an interactional model that characterises the teaching-learning process most appropriately.*

Schaffer, 1996, p.26

LEV VYGOTSKY

The two figures who were to exert the most influence on later 20th century educational thinking and practice, Piaget and Vygotsky, were both born in the same year, 1896, but their life experiences were radically different. Vygotsky lived through huge political upheaval in Russia, and this affected his ability to work and to disseminate his ideas. A brilliant scholar from an early age, he studied medicine and law as well as history and philosophy, before coming to wider recognition for his work on developmental psychology. His writings embrace ideas drawn from art, poetry and theatre as well as scientific principles. His main interests lay in the relationship of language to thought processes, and the social origin of cognitive skills.

Although he died in 1934, Vygotsky's writings did not gain wide recognition until much later, as they were suppressed for over 20 years after his death. Central to his ideas was the belief that cognitive development takes place in a social context, and therefore interactions are essential for such development to take place. Perhaps most relevant to the discussion of high ability is his concept of the Zone of Proximal Development (ZPD), where cognitive progress can occur. This is the zone where a problem is posed which is too difficult for the child to work out alone, but capable of being solved with the help of someone more competent, and it illustrates how crucial the role of 'teacher' is in Vygotskian theory. However, the ideal learning environment is characterised here as a fairly intensive one-to-one interaction, which would be difficult to achieve on a regular basis with all children in a busy classroom. It is clear that others have a key role to play, whether parents, older siblings, classroom assistants, mentors, tutors – anyone who is able to spend time with a child. Schaffer describes such interactions as 'joint involvement episodes' (1996) and characterises them thus:

> .... *following on from Vygotsky it appears that such encounters, in which children can make their first attempts at some new skill on the basis of the adult's support and feedback, provide the requisite context for the growth of higher cognitive functions generally.*

Schaffer (1996) p.236

Perhaps the most significant challenge Vygotsky poses to much current educational practice is the way he confronts the culture of testing which, he says, focuses on '*the yesterday of a child's development*' (quoted in Palmer and Dolya, 2004). Rather, he advocates, '*the only good kind of instruction is that which marches ahead of development, and leads it*' (ibid).

JEROME BRUNER

Many education professionals all over the world have been inspired and challenged by the ideas of Bruner, whose seminal work 'The Process of Education' in 1960 made an international impact. In this book he states the now legendary hypothesis 'that any subject can be taught effectively in some intellectually honest form to any child at any stage of development.' He goes on, later in the book, to say that the pursuit of excellence should not be limited to gifted students, but neither should teaching be aimed at the average student. '*The quest ... is to devise materials that will challenge the superior student while not destroying the confidence and will-to-learn [of the others].*' He argues for the teaching in the early years of many basic principles of science and mathematics, in order to lay a better foundation for the revisiting of these subjects later. This he calls the 'spiral curriculum'.

Bruner's later research and writings build on and develop these ideas and he has contributed much to the debate on teaching and learning. It is impossible in this short summary to do justice to his ideas, such as those on 'scaffolding' learning (Wood *et al*, 1976), on children's talk and language acquisition (Bruner, 1983) and his emphasis on humanity and creativity in the curriculum which continues to have a major significance for many practitioners in the educational world today. Gardner sums it up thus: '*Jerome Bruner is not merely one of the foremost educational thinkers of our era; he is also an inspired learner and teacher. His infectious curiosity inspires all who are not completely jaded.*' (2001).

MARGARET DONALDSON

Donaldson's influential book 'Children's Minds', published in 1978, builds on, challenges and re-interprets some of Piaget's key theories, particularly relating to young children and their capabilities. With inspiration from Vygotsky and Bruner (among others), she discusses the context of children's meaning-making, and shows that young children's skills and abilities in thought and language are often under-estimated and therefore under-valued when they come into school. She looks at factors that influence success in school, and how to avoid the disenchantment that comes from feeling bored or a failure. Building on the view of children as competent learners capable of creative thought, she emphasises the importance of teaching to help children achieve their intellectual potential, without losing the 'warm-bloodedness' they have naturally as young children.

Here is a brief selection of key texts relevant to this chapter, for further reading and research.

Bruner, J.S. (1971) *The Relevance of Education*, New York: Norton.

Dewey, J. (1897) *My Pedagogic Creed*. The School Journal vol. 54 (January) pp. 77–80.

Dewey, J. (1938) *Experience and Education*. New York: Collier Books. (Collier edition first published 1963).

Donaldson, M. (1978) *Children's Minds*. Glasgow, Fontana.

Gruber, H.E. and Vonëche, J.J. (1995, 2nd edn.) *The Essential Piaget: An Interpretive Reference and Guide.* Northvale, NJ: Jason Aronsen.

Lilley, I. (ed.) (1967) *Friedrich Froebel: A selection from his writings.* Cambridge: Cambridge University Press.

Montessori, Maria (1917) *The Advanced Montessori Method (Vol. 1: Spontaneous Activity in Education; Vol. 2: The Montessori Elementary Material).* New York: Frederick A. Stokes & Co.

Vygotsky, L.S. (1978) *Mind in society*. Cambridge, MA: Harvard University Press.

Vygotsky, L.S. (1985) *Thought and Language*. Cambridge, MA: The M.I.T. Press.

CHAPTER 3

IDENTIFICATION

WHY IDENTIFY SPECIAL ABILITIES?

It has been argued by some professionals working in the field of high ability that identification is unnecessary, as, given a sufficiently enriched environment and lots of appropriate opportunities, children will flourish and receive all the stimulation and encouragement they need. This is probably true, and applicable both to special needs and special abilities, but very few structured educational settings are able to provide such an environment. Of course this should be the goal, especially in the early years, but the truth is that resources and staffing are always limited to some degree, and even more so once formal schooling begins. Some sort of prioritisation is therefore necessary, in order to meet learning needs in the best possible way.

This does not mean that hard and fast identification is necessary or desirable, especially in the early years when children's development varies so considerably. Provision of the widest possible opportunities for exploration and discovery can lead to the recognition of many different types of special ability. Children cannot demonstrate their emerging abilities in particular areas if they do not have the opportunity. It is important to observe as much in free play situations as in more structured activity, as children may demonstrate capabilities above or beyond what is expected, or in different ways (for example inventing a complicated game or showing fascination with complex patterns).

IDENTIFICATION METHODS

Opportunities to learn about the children can easily be missed if provision is not made for identifying their special abilities. You do not need to provide an onerous task, more a way of thinking and enquiry that can permeate many kinds of activity. An example from the author's own observations might serve to illustrate how this could be done.

In a nursery setting within a large primary school, children were being assessed on their knowledge of the names of shapes. In order to do this, a hand-drawn chart was used similar to the one on p.19. However, the children only had to identify a circle, a triangle, a square and a rectangle, and there was no possibility within the framework for discovering whether the children knew any more shapes. A more open-ended assessment might uncover some surprising knowledge. There are several ways this could be done, perhaps by asking the children who have successfully named the four prescribed shapes if they know any others, or perhaps by having more pictures of shapes available to see if they can recognise them.

Assessment, of course, is only a snapshot of a particular moment. The example above can lead on to creative and stimulating games involving more complicated shapes, as many children will like to hear some of the more unusual names, such as rhombus or crescent. Four-year-old Ahmed, for example, had a much-loved game which he would play over and over again with his mother. She would draw a shape on a small magic drawing board (of the type which is easily erased and reused over and over again) which she kept hidden from view, for him to guess, and he would love the challenge of the more uncommon shapes. His favourite shape was a trapezium. Soon after his mother initiated the game, he wanted to take a turn to draw the shapes himself for her to guess, thus practising important skills. This game could easily be adapted for group or whole-class activities, and would suit all abilities as a wide variety of shapes could be drawn. The class could pick one of the more unusual ones as 'shape of the week', and use it in lots of different ways (for example in making patterns, or counting how many in a picture).

This is only one example of how both assessment and classroom practice can accommodate a wide variety of abilities, curiosities

Name	Circle	Triangle	Square	Rectangle
Katy				
Ahmed				
William				
Sara				
Callum				
Tia				
Niamh				
Conor				
Chloe				
Ayisha				
Ryan				
Bethany				
Jodhan				

Figure 2: Example of chart used to test children's knowledge of names of shapes

and interests, at the same time contributing to identification of special abilities in an inclusive way. It is important to think about where and how assessment currently takes place in all types of activity (for example in role play, PE, art and craft, music, social awareness, block play and many others), and whether children are given opportunities to go beyond the confines of any particular assessment framework.

In order to include the widest possible spectrum of activities, information should also be gathered from the home environment about special abilities. Any educational environment, however enriched, is by its nature artificial and will not provide the same stimuli as home. Parents are often able to spend quality one-to-one time with their children, and usually know them better than anyone else. A routine question on admission forms about special abilities as well as special needs would provide valuable additional information to what can be observed and recorded in the classroom (see *Chapter 10* for more suggestions on working with parents).

The idea of identification through provision has been developed by Freeman (1998) who advocates what she calls a 'sports approach'. This is a reference to the way in which identification of sporting ability is often undertaken, where artificial limits are not placed on children's achievement, but they are encouraged to perform to their natural limits and then to work on surpassing those.

One interesting framework for identification which is suitable for use in the early years is the Nebraska Starry Night Protocol (it is used, for example, in the Chelsea Open-Air Nursery which was founded by Susan Isaacs and continues to be rewarded with accolades for outstanding early years practice – see Counsell (2004a) for further details). A description can be found in Eyre (1997) with an illustration of the various categories included in the framework.

A useful chapter ('Who says she's gifted?') with further discussion of different approaches to identification, including those mentioned above, can be found in Hymer and Michel (2002). Hymer advocates an inclusive approach to identification, embracing the principle of identifying through provision, and goes on to discuss the use of facilitated reflection for the learners and the role of the teacher. Picking up on ideas put forward by Gardner (1983), Wallace (2000) and Reis *et al.* (1994), he introduces the concepts of a stimulus lesson, a learning dispositions log and an interest audit, as well as a sample parents' questionnaire and multiple intelligences profile.

The important challenge relating to the issue of identification is how to recognise and support children's widely varying abilities and talents within the context of school or nursery, within what can appear to be insurmountable curriculum constraints and with limited resources and staffing. When policy and practice are moulded to nurture individual strengths rather than some arbitrary cut-off point or percentage, identification will become a valuable tool that serves the needs of children and teachers, and not the other way round.

A note is important here about the children's differing abilities in all kinds of fields such as sport, music, drama, art, mechanics, environmental awareness and many others. Because of the limited scope of this book, many abilities have not been given the discussion they deserve. Teachers are encouraged to look for and celebrate as many diverse abilities as possible, and to collect as much information from home as possible. There are many sources of information and helpful contacts for teachers in areas such as music, art and sport (see for example the *'useful websites'* section at the end of this book), and where a particular ability goes beyond the expertise of the teacher, it is very important to find specialist help so that a child can be nurtured and encouraged, especially if this is not happening outside school.

CHAPTER 4

SOME POSSIBLE DIFFICULTIES FOR CHILDREN WITH SPECIAL ABILITIES

CASE STUDY

Miriam is seven years old. She has not had an easy experience of school life so far. In reception class she found it difficult to relate to other children, and had frequent emotional outbursts of screaming when things did not go the way she wanted. Her high ability in several areas was acknowledged by the school. She joined Year 1 for literacy, and spent half an hour a week discussing science with a boy in Year 6, which they both enjoyed. Her teacher was very sympathetic and, with the extra adult help available in reception, Miriam had a reasonable year, though it was never easy. In Year 1, however, things fell apart. A less experienced teacher, combined with circumstances which prevented Miriam from joining the Year 2 literacy class, made things much more difficult, and to add to this the older boy had now left the school and there was not so much adult help available. Miriam developed symptoms of stress and was frequently absent. When in school, her behaviour was at times unmanageable and the school struggled to find ways to meet her ability needs, as these were uneven. For example, although she could read and discuss at an extremely high level for her age, she found handwriting a slow and difficult process. She also struggled with social relationships in her peer group. Her parents considered taking her out of school on many occasions, but she desperately wanted to stay as she had a burning desire to be 'like a normal child'. However, in Year 2 the situation did not improve, and Miriam left the school and was home-educated for a time.

Research findings are somewhat contradictory in judging whether highly able children experience more emotional, behavioural and social problems than other groups of children. There is not really any conclusive evidence to suggest that this is true. Indeed, some children are socially extremely able and can use their intelligence to their advantage, both in school and in other social contexts. However, where more able children are having emotional, social or behavioural problems, as Miriam was, our understanding of the child's ability can help us to find ways to support the child and begin to improve the situation. Evidence from the NAGC helpline suggests that where more able children do experience difficulties in these areas, there are certain patterns and characteristics (usually linked to the interaction of the child within a particular environment) which occur commonly across a wide variety of children. These are presented here in order to help teachers to recognise and understand the behaviours that can result. Further valuable discussion can be found in Leyden (2002) on the human needs of children, including those with exceptional abilities.

There is no such thing as a typical highly able child. Therefore, there is no one solution that will help all children who are experiencing difficulties. Each child is a unique and complex interaction of personality, temperament, ability and environment. Problems can arise when these factors combine in certain ways, resulting in imbalance and frustration. The outlines given here can combine in any one child, and may intensify or decrease depending on circumstances and also on maturity.

THE 'OUT-OF-SYNC' CHILD

A five-year-old girl is playing chess very happily with her brother who is three years older. As she is very good at chess, she beats him. Her mother comes into the room to tell her that it is time for bed, and all of a sudden she throws an explosive temper tantrum because she has to go to bed before her brother.

In this scenario, the girl's behaviour can be seen at different levels. First, her intellectual ability and reasoning are advanced for her chronological age, allowing her to beat her brother at chess. Second, her physical needs are those of a five-year-old, so she has to go to bed earlier than her brother. Third, her emotional state when frustrated leads her to behave like a younger child and throw a temper tantrum.

All children have variations in these levels to some degree or another, but in a highly able child these can be quite pronounced, especially at a very young age. If a four-year-old boy, for example, has some of the mental abilities of an average seven-year-old, this is nearly twice his age, and the imbalance with some of his other abilities (eg. motor skills) or emotional age may well lead to intense frustration at times. Teachers may find it confusing when a child can reason at a level that seems almost adult, but the next minute behave in an extremely childish way. It is important to remember that this is perfectly normal, and that all children need to be silly and childish at times without our expectations becoming a burden to them.

THE 'SOCIAL MISFIT'

As mentioned earlier, some children have particular social abilities, and many highly able children use their intelligence to find good ways to fit in and make friends (ironically this can sometimes involve disguising their ability to some degree). All children vary in social ability, which may or may not be linked to other ability areas. It is an issue of vital importance to a successful school career, as school is above all a social context, where everything is done in interaction and relationships are crucial. The child that does not fit in socially is at risk of lowered self-esteem and also of many negative long-term consequences (see for example Schaffer, 1996). There are reasons why some very able children struggle in this area, and several possible explanations as to why this might happen to children in the early years of school are outlined here.

First there is the child who is passionately interested in a particular subject, such as butterflies or outer space. Many bright children develop these intense fascinations from a very young age, often moving to a new curiosity when one topic (or their parent or teacher) is exhausted. The difficulty comes when they try to share their enthusiasm with others, who are not in the slightest bit interested and may find the subject rather strange. For children who may already be insecure in a new setting (nursery or school) this may feel like rejection, not only of the topic in question but also of themselves. They may start to feel different, and this feeling may be reinforced by the behaviour of the other children.

Other highly able children have a burning desire to be the leader in any game that is being played. They sometimes make up rules of incredible sophistication which lead to other children rapidly losing interest and finding other friends to play with. This can result in children being labelled as bossy or pushy, and they may also feel rejected by others.

Another factor can be the level of language used by a child who has developed further in this particular area than others. A highly articulate three-year-old does not yet have the social awareness to relate well with children who do not speak at the same level, and therefore may become frustrated or seek attention from older children or adults.

Of course some children, having experienced an initial negative reaction, will quickly learn to keep some areas of interest or complex rule-making for home only, and find successful ways to integrate at school. The children at risk of social isolation are the ones who cannot successfully do this, and may perceive the games, interests or conversation of the other children as babyish. They may be desperate to fit in and make friends, but their repeated attempts may be unsuccessful, and over time they may begin to feel there is something wrong with them. For others it is not such a problem; they may be content to be on their own sometimes, as long as the other children do not give them a difficult time. But given the current emphasis within Foundation Stage on social competence, such a child may be labelled as socially inadequate from an early age.

Observations of children interacting in other situations, outside school, perhaps with older children or with those who share their interests, could give a totally different picture. Opportunities to mix across age groups and with others of similar ability, perhaps in common interest groups or mini-mentoring schemes, may help children to realise there are those with whom they can relate more easily, and that the problem is more one of mismatch in the highly artificial environment of school than a specific problem within themselves.

THE BORED CHILD

Boredom is an extremely useful human reaction. If we were not capable of being bored, then we would never have the motivation to achieve anything. The problem in school is that children are not often in control of the solution to their boredom – to find something more interesting to do. Thus they may find it difficult to engage with classroom activities, but powerless to do anything about it. In the early years, children are egocentric beings who do not understand the concept of a curriculum imposed by an adult, or why they should do certain things if they do not want to. Many bright children are developing strong ideas of their own, and yet are still only young, and likely to tip over into frustration very easily if things don't go according to their plan.

Many very able children dislike repetition of things which are already familiar, and find it difficult to deal with in a classroom context, for example at 'carpet time'. They may respond by fidgeting, or getting up and wandering around, or daydreaming or looking out of the window. Some of these behaviours are more disruptive than others, and more likely to lead to labelling of a child as 'difficult'.

Even adults react with annoyance if people try to teach them things they already know – they may be much more polite about it, depending on the context, but are liable at the very least to mutter to their friends or colleagues. One example of this took place in the author's own experience at a school where a newly-appointed headteacher addressed everyone at a staff meeting and proceeded to give a lecture on basic developments in education over the last hundred years or so. As they were all trained teachers and had covered this material during training, it felt unnecessary and patronising. Children don't have the same degree of tact and diplomacy as adults, but feel just as strongly and are liable to react in a much more honest way.

Professor Dr Ferre Laevers in his work on children in the early years at Leuven University has developed the concept of Involvement Scales (Laevers, undated) with which a child's involvement in the activities provided can be measured. This is used to evaluate whether the setting (nursery, pre-school or reception class) is providing appropriately for the children in its care. The Effective Early Learning programme has been developed in Britain in response to and as a further development of Professor Laevers' work, and provides training for early years educators in using involvement scales for professional evaluation (see http://www.worc.ac.uk/businessandresearch/specialist/1028.html for more details).

This method of evaluation starts from the premise that if a child of any ability is not engaged and involved in an activity, it is the provision which needs careful scrutiny, not the child.

Young children are programmed to be curious, to explore, to discover. This is just as true of highly able children, who need varied activities which are challenging and enjoyable, capable of engaging and sustaining their interest.

THE PERFECTIONIST

Children of all abilities can have perfectionist tendencies, and there does not seem to be any conclusive research evidence that able children are more perfectionist as a group than others. However, when the perfectionist child is also highly able, there can be specific problems which cause difficulty for parents and educators.

The first concern is the child who cannot complete anything, as it is never good enough. This child makes a tiny error and the whole page is ripped up in frustration. A smudge on a piece of artwork leads to an explosive temper tantrum, which seems an enormous overreaction to such a small mistake. Another child is dismayed because a piece of early writing does not look like the neat print in a book.

Other children develop an aversion to taking any kind of risk, whether physical or mental. They are happy and safe with what they know they can do, and are unwilling to face the chance that they might make a mistake or fail in some way. They may be nervous about new experiences or a change in routine, as it threatens their security of what is known and well understood.

Perfectionism is not in itself a harmful thing, and there are some appropriate outlets for it where children can be encouraged to do a task perfectly (for example doing a jigsaw puzzle or working out a sum). But much learning takes place when children are making mistakes. These are inevitable when children are exploring new concepts and working in the 'Zone of Proximal Development' described by Vygotsky (see *Chapter 2*). Mistakes should be seen as normal, expected, at times even celebrated. (This does not apply to silly slips which can often be ignored.) We all continue to make mistakes throughout our lives, and to learn from them. Curriculum developments of recent years which have led to a high degree of emphasis on the 'right answer' are not helpful in teaching children how to learn, how to experiment and how to take risks. Rather, they can reinforce a perfectionist child's view that 'it has to be right'. A child who is getting everything right all the time is not a child who is learning, however good it may look on a school report. A classroom where it is normal and safe to take a risk will help children grow and develop into effective and independent learners.

This may be an appropriate place to mention the importance of risk-taking for teachers in the classroom. It is not only children who need to learn to step out of their comfort zones. It is true that the educational climate in recent years has not necessarily facilitated the ideal conditions for taking risks (although as this book is being written there are welcome signs that this might be improving in developments such as the Creative Curriculum and projects such as Creative Partnerships), but in order to meet the needs of very different children it is important to think round and beyond the curriculum, especially in relation to children with special abilities or needs.

LEARNING DIFFICULTIES

It is not possible in this book to give a thorough or in-depth examination of children with special abilities who also have learning difficulties. Readers are referred to Montgomery (2003) for a fuller and more detailed account which looks at a wide range of learning difficulties and special needs. There is also an excellent chapter on dyslexia in Stopper (2000). The issues affecting highly able children with learning difficulties has been a rather neglected area of study in Britain until recently, and many teachers may not be aware of the particular problems which can occur for bright children if there are also obstacles which make learning in school difficult for them.

A survey of the membership of NAGC, conducted in 1999, indicated that between 5 and 10% of children represented by these families had some kind of learning difficulty. These included dyslexia, dyspraxia, attention-deficit hyperactivity disorder (ADHD) and Asperger syndrome. This is obviously a rather unrepresentative sample (around 2,500 families, who were self-selecting as they had joined a national organisation), but it does indicate that a significant number of children who have special abilities may also have difficulties which make certain sorts of learning very challenging for them.

The most widespread learning difficulty reported among more able children is dyslexia, and it is now generally acknowledged that many dyslexic people have special abilities of one sort or another. These are still not always recognised in school, however, as there is such a great emphasis in the early years on developing literacy skills, so for the bright dyslexic child school can be a place where weaknesses are highlighted but there is little recognition of areas of strength. By the time other skills (maybe in art, design technology, ICT or drama) begin to be recognised and valued by school, it may be too late for some children, as they have decided school has little to offer them. This negative experience may have been compounded for some highly able children whose learning needs have also not been recognised, and have therefore felt a failure for being unable to produce work of sufficient quantity or to a high enough standard. Alternatively, they may have been considered of average ability, leading to intense frustration. Spelling or handwriting difficulties may have been attributed to lack of effort rather than a genuine difficulty. The effect of all this on self-esteem in the crucial early years in school cannot be underestimated, and while a well-known few seem to have the resilience of character to come through and achieve great things (almost despite their school experiences), many others must surely fall by the wayside.

The important challenge for a teacher is to provide opportunities so that the widest possible range of special abilities can be recognised and then supported. In one nursery setting, the teachers facilitated creative play (especially for boys) by combining role-play toys (eg. dressing-up clothes, small world figures) with building blocks. One boy, who had been recognised as having significant learning difficulties in a variety of verbal tasks, built a washing machine for the clothes, complete with all the pipes and plumbing attachments. This was an outstanding achievement for a four-year-old, and this particular ability was recorded and photographed. It is to be hoped that in the later school years, particularly when the environment becomes somewhat less flexible in Years 1 and 2, that a way can be found for these special abilities to be nurtured and valued.

We have seen in this chapter some of the possible difficulties which may be experienced by children with special abilities. It has to be emphasised that being bright does not necessarily lead to problems; however, many of the difficulties described above can be exacerbated by a school system which is inflexible and does not recognise individual needs of all kinds. Our goal in educating young children should be to help each one to flourish in the best way possible, not to put obstacles in their way or make life harder than it needs to be for them and their families. Looking for strengths, rather than concentrating on weaknesses, can make a positive difference to a child's sense of self worth, and consequently the child's view of the education system as a whole.

CHAPTER 5

THE GENDER DEBATE

CASE STUDIES

Rebecca, 6

Rebecca, aged six, demonstrated her high ability from an extremely early age. She could read fluently by the age of three and she loved organised and structured activities. She was desperate to start 'big school' and her favourite game was playing school with her little sister. Rebecca's mother was concerned that the nursery was not meeting her daughter's need for a structured learning environment, and as Rebecca's birthday was in early September formal schooling seemed a long way off. She made enquiries about the possibility of Rebecca starting school a year early and, after some searching, found a small village infant school willing to take her. Her experience at this school has been extremely positive, and she is a confident and articulate little girl looking forward to transferring to junior school.

Jack, 5

Jack, aged five, is the third child in his family. He has two older sisters who are recognised as highly able and have been given special provision in their primary school. His mother feels Jack is also very bright, but is not showing it in the same way that the girls did. She was apprehensive about his entry to reception class, even though the class size was very small and the school very supportive. At the end of his first year, he has had a mixed experience, as he did not take well to structured activities, often finding a completely different way to do something. At times he seemed highly uncooperative, but was often very creative. He had a particular problem with handwriting, and it took some carefully thought out strategies to encourage him to write, even though his writing was actually reasonably competent for his age. His mother is still concerned that he is finding the school experience difficult and negative at times and she worries that, as work becomes more formal in the next few years, his individuality and creativity will not be encouraged or find room to flourish.

Aline, 5

Aline is a bright five-year-old who is delightful at home, although she has never slept much and continues to ask difficult questions well into the evening, which can be exhausting. However, she did not have serious problems until she started nursery, where she became extremely frustrated and started to lash out aggressively at teachers and other students. A lack of understanding about where the frustration might be coming from resulted in her being labelled as a severe problem child, and spending the majority of the time at nursery isolated from the other children and desperately unhappy. A small, supportive reception class with a more creative approach has helped her, and she now participates in class activities to some degree, but she remains volatile and her mother is extremely concerned about her future in school.

Alex, 5

Alex, aged five, has just completed reception class. He is a fluent reader with a developing competence in maths, and enjoys reading many different books (Harry Potter is his current favourite). At school he is co-operative and eager to please his teacher. He often repeats her instructions to the other children if he feels they are doing something wrong. He sometimes joins in with the boys who play football at break time, but often prefers to play with the girls. At home he likes writing stories, drawing pictures and any art or craft activity.

Any discussion of the complex issues of gender is fraught with dangers of generalisation and over-simplification. However, differences between girls and boys in the early years can affect many aspects of school life (for example see Browne, 1991), and there is research evidence that children reinforce gender roles at a very early age through adults, through peer influences and through the stories and texts they encounter (see for example Davies and Banks, 1992). The extent to which such differences are innate or learned behaviour is a debate beyond the scope of this book (for an interesting summary of some of the relevant research regarding high ability and gender, see Freeman, 2000), but where differences do exist, it is important to acknowledge their possible effects so that every child can have the best possible experience.

It is an interesting statistic that, during at least the last six years when reliable records have been kept, the numbers of calls to the NAGC helpline concerning boys are consistently twice as numerous as those about girls. As we saw previously, the majority of calls to the helpline take place when children are in the early years, between three and seven. Assuming an equal number of highly able girls and boys (although statistics for early testing consistently identify girls as more able – see, for example, DfES

2004 where girls outperform boys in nearly all areas of the national tests), this seems to point to highly able boys experiencing more problems of one sort of another in the crucial early years at nursery and school. There are also differences in the type of problem discussed on the helpline. Calls about specific problems are many and varied, and not all occur frequently enough to categorise. Of those that do, boys outnumber girls in behaviour problems, handwriting concerns, learning difficulties and lack of acknowledgement by the school of a child's ability. These statistics show more than double incidence for boys, to allow for the already higher number of boys represented. Handwriting difficulties mentioned in helpline calls for boys, for example, outnumber those mentioned for girls by eight to one.

In the light of the above figures, it is noteworthy that in the research literature from journals specialising in giftedness there are many articles on gifted women and girls, usually focusing on secondary age or into higher education (see for example Reis and Callahan, 1996), and a number on gender differences (eg. Jacobs and Weisz, 1994) but hardly any on the subject of gifted boys, particularly in the early years. One interesting research study looking at academically able boys is Power *et al* (1998) but it focuses on older students. The shortage of studies relating to highly able young boys in gifted and other educational journals may reflect the fact that the discipline of gender studies has in the past focused mainly on the experiences of girls and women, and only relatively recently has the balance shifted somewhat to explore masculinities as well. It seems clear that further research is needed in this area.

With somewhere in the region of two and a half thousand calls and enquiries a year, the helpline is obviously only a small indicator and cannot be taken as representative. It also cannot be stressed enough that parents are only likely to call a helpline if they perceive there is a problem of some sort, so these statistics do not include the majority of more able children who are happy in school. But the experience of those more able children who are not happy in school can be extremely valuable, and this book is intended to highlight some potential issues to consider. It is likely, too, that many other parents are experiencing similar difficulties but do not feel able to call a national helpline, or know of its existence. The consistency of the statistics regarding gender over a five-year period, which has seen extensive changes in the national strategy for gifted and talented children, may give a pointer towards ways we can help both girls and boys to have a more positive experience, not just in their school lives but beyond.

A cursory glance through literature on parenting skills at the local library or bookshop reveals an increasing number of titles relating specifically to girls or boys which discuss differences between them (for example Biddulph 1997, Hartley-Brewer 2000). It is also now impossible to escape the yearly outcry in the media when yet again girls outperform boys in public examinations. When it comes to highly able young children, we need to examine carefully the factors that can affect their school experience in the crucial early years.

For boys, as noted above, all early test results show them to be achieving less highly than girls on a range of tests (DfES, 2004). The differences are most noticeable in the area of literacy and verbal skills, and if, for example, Key Stage 1 results are compared in the writing task for 2004, especially among the higher achievers (above level 2b and at level 3), the contrast is striking (ibid). This raises a serious question about early forms of testing, as there seems to be some sort of inbuilt disadvantage for bright boys, who may be less likely to be identified at this stage. Of course there are many concerns about assessment and testing, some raised elsewhere in this book, but where judgements are written down (whether this is Stepping Stones, baseline testing, Foundation Stage profiling, or Key Stage 1 assessment or tests or any other measure used with young children) it is important to realise their limitations. What is measured is largely imposed on teachers and does not take account of the different abilities and talents a child might demonstrate. Children can only show a particular ability if given an opportunity, so if this is not expected or looked for, the result could be an under-assessment. The teacher only sees the children in the context of school, where they could under-perform in classroom assessments or tests for any number of reasons (including stress, boredom, frustration, anxiety or unfamiliarity). The question is, why do bright boys appear to be under-performing more than bright girls, and what it is possible to do in the everyday classroom to mitigate the effects of this?

The helpline statistics quoted above may give us a clue. The chief areas of concern where boys outnumbered girls were behaviour issues, handwriting problems and learning difficulties. These factors often seem to lead to the school not recognising or acknowledging that a child is bright. These issues are covered in more detail elsewhere in this book, but it is important to note here that teacher reactions to these concerns may disadvantage both boys and girls in different ways.

One possible reaction is to say 'Boys will be boys', and to expect lower standards of work and behaviour from the boys because that is how they are. This attitude does not look at the possible reasons for these lower standards or find ways of enabling the boys to do better (and probably some of the girls too). A more creative approach to writing in the case study above, for example, enabled Jack to show that he could write creatively in a motivating and meaningful context. Suggested strategies for encouraging reluctant writers are given in *Chapter 6*. It is also important to look at learning styles (see Smith, 1998), particularly of kinaesthetic and visual-spatial learners who find it impossible to learn by sitting still and listening, but who may show huge improvements in their learning when more appropriate methods are used. This also applies to children with learning difficulties, which may not be apparent if they are very bright (see *Chapter 4*).

Another reaction is to invest large amounts of time and effort into disciplining those perceived as 'problem boys' (usually a small minority of the class) to behave and conform to classroom expectations. The boys gain attention from this, but much of it is negative. Where it is positive, it may be rewarding behaviour such as sitting still or completing a line of writing, rather than recognising a creative idea or spark of brilliance. The children who get on with their work quietly and co-operate with instructions are given much less attention in this scenario, and this can have the opposite effect to that intended, as they realise that the only certain way to get teacher attention is to misbehave.

Of course, many boys do not have behaviour problems or other difficulties, and some are well integrated and flourish in their class. Boys who are sensitive and artistic may find school a difficult place for very different reasons, however, if they struggle to relate to other boys. They may prefer to spend time alone or with some of the girls, and as they get older may find that they are teased or socially isolated. This can be a humiliating experience which can affect self-esteem for the rest of their school career and beyond. It may also leave them more vulnerable to bullying, so it is vitally important to have strategies in every classroom to help all the children feel valued and able to appreciate one another. Creative approaches such as the effective use of circle time, puppets and stories can help, and these need to be reflected in the whole school ethos, including careful thought about break times and lunch times when anti-social behaviour can occur.

Where girls exhibit behaviour that is more commonly associated with boys, they may be disadvantaged in the classroom. Teachers who accept a certain boisterousness or lack of conformity in boys may discourage the same behaviour in girls or react more strongly to it. Behaviour that is assertive may be interpreted as cheeky or defiant, and any display of knowledge may be regarded as showing-off. As some of the response may be at a subconscious level, it is important for teachers to examine their practice very carefully, perhaps with the help of an observer to focus on a specific aspect of their teaching, or by video-recording themselves in action.

Although statistics show girls outperforming boys at just about every level in national examinations, the subsequent career prospects of high-achieving girls are not necessarily in line with the expectations that these results might indicate. Although there has been an improvement, it is still difficult for women to aspire to the highest positions in many professions. It is interesting to speculate whether the value that is placed in school on conformity and working to the test (to achieve the best results) might actually be doing many girls a disservice further down the line. The qualities of individuality, nonconformity and the ability and willingness to question authority are not always appreciated in school, but often prove useful attributes for success in later life.

There is really no substitute for dealing with all children individually, whether boys or girls, and looking at each one's unique capabilities, temperament and personality. Awareness, however, of children's own developing perceptions of gender roles and norms, and the influence that adults can have on these, will help in the enhancement of classroom practice so that every child can flourish and be valued.

CHAPTER 6

HANDWRITING

CASE STUDIES

Luke, 7

Luke is a bright and articulate seven-year-old boy in year 2 who is fascinated by science, electronics and gadgets of any sort. He designs machines using intricate detailed drawings, and his class teacher allows him to do this at carpet time, otherwise he can become extremely restless. She has discovered that he can draw and listen at the same time. His mother is very concerned about her son's lack of progress in school, and worries that he seems very unhappy there. He hates writing anything down as it interferes with his thought processes, and though his handwriting does not look unreasonable for a boy of his age, it is rather slow and laboured.

At his mother's request he was observed in class during year 2. The class was engaged in a writing activity, having been visited by an author the day before. The task was to imagine a pair of shoes that would take you to any time you wanted to visit, and describe the adventures you had. The observer felt that Luke would enjoy this task, as it seemed to give much scope to the imagination he clearly took pleasure in using. However, about half way through the allotted time, he had only written a couple of lines, which were the opening given on the board. The observer asked him if he had any ideas for how the story would develop. It became clear that he was toying in his mind with two different scenarios, one which would take him back to the dawn of the industrial age, when there were many ground-breaking inventions and discoveries. The other scenario would take him forward to the age when he imagined robots would rule the world. Both ideas were vividly described to the observer, who wished she had been able to tape record the conversation. The teacher would never have discovered any of this rich thinking, however, as by the end of the session there was still very little written in his exercise book.

Leonie, 7

Seven-year-old Leonie started school at four years old and, according to her mother, was a child full of energy and curiosity, who asked deep and challenging questions and wanted to learn about everything. Within a short time of starting at school, however, her mother noticed a gradual change in her. She was becoming withdrawn and unhappy, and had stopped asking so many questions. Her mother became particularly alarmed one day, in her second term at school, when they were discussing school, and Leonie said that she was stupid. In conversation with her teacher, it became evident that there was a particular emphasis on developing handwriting skills, and that Leonie was struggling with this. As she was very able and a good reader, she had been put in a group with some other very able girls, and it became evident that she was comparing himself with them. Most of them were a few months older, and were not having the same difficulties with writing. These early experiences seemed to set the tone for Leonie's dislike of handwriting, which has persisted through Years 1 and 2. She has many creative thoughts, but finds it nearly impossible to get them down on paper. At home, her mother has bought a Dictaphone which helps with homework, but in school the problems continue.

The rationale for this chapter is the large number of calls received on the NAGC Helpline where handwriting is a factor in a child's unhappiness or dislike of school. There seems, however, little documentation of the problem or of the relevant issues in literature relating to high ability. As a result of this, NAGC has carried out a study looking into some of the issues in more depth, both for schools and for individual children, with funding from the DfES. Some of the material in this chapter is taken from this study, which can be obtained in full from NAGC.

Difficulties with handwriting can have very different origins, and they can affect more able children just as much as others. The assumptions that all highly able children will easily develop clear, legible handwriting, or that neat handwriting is linked with intelligence, are totally false. Some very able pupils do acquire excellent handwriting skills from an early age, but there are also many who find the whole business of handwriting extremely challenging. Changes brought about by the National Curriculum in recent years do not appear to have helped, as handwriting is now a major focus in Key Stage 1, and this can produce extra stress for children whose fine motor skills may not yet be sufficiently developed to write well.

The act of handwriting is a complex physical skill. Children develop physically at different rates, so perhaps it is not surprising that some will struggle with writing at first. There has been little observation or recording as to why some highly able children continue to have difficulties, and the emotional and psychological effects of these experiences.

A FRENCH EXPERIMENT

At one infant school, Herne Infants in the south-east of England, a teacher was struck by the differences between French children who were six or seven years old, and those in Years 1 and 2 at her own school. The French children were writing in a fluent and joined style, and few were experiencing difficulty with this. In England, joined writing was seen as an advanced skill, and many children struggled with it.

The teacher was so impressed by the differences that she obtained some funding to study practice in French schools further. She discovered that the foundations for writing skills are laid in the 'école maternelle', which children attend from the ages of three to six. In France, writing is seen as a complex skill to master, and so a great deal of structured time and activity goes into preparing for it. It is seen as having elements of physical education and of art, so children are taken through carefully sequenced gross motor activities such as rolling and twisting, as well as practising fine motor skills in patterning activities on paper. These lay the foundation for letter-writing, which is not introduced until later. When it is, fluid joined movements are practised from the start, and the preparation ensures that most children succeed with them.

The findings of this study were written up (Thomas, 1997) and there was a flurry of interest in the British press. However, in many schools here the practice has not changed, despite obvious advantages of the French approach (suitably adapted for use in British schools). At Herne Infants, however, practice has been revolutionised. From reception, children begin a programme of physical activities designed to underpin successful development of handwriting, and practise patterning skills in a number of different and enjoyable ways. Towards the end of the year writing is introduced, and this is joined from the start. Physical exercises and patterning activities continue in subsequent years (for example in Year 2 the children regularly draw patterns to different kinds of music using coloured felt-tipped pens). By the end of Key Stage 1 most children are writing fluently and easily.

GENDER AND HANDWRITING

As seen in *Chapter 5*, gender is an issue which appears to affect handwriting. Out of calls to the NAGC helpline which mentioned handwriting as a factor, concerns about boys outnumbered those about girls by eight to one. The problems more able boys appear to face with writing may, at least in part, be linked to slower development of fine motor skills. Observation in nursery and reception settings would also suggest that where choice is available, boys generally do not choose the activities which involve development of these fine motor skills, such as cutting out or threading. So not only do many girls develop these skills earlier, they may also practise them more.

It was also seen in *Chapter 5* that these patterns continue, with a marked contrast between the results of more able boys and girls in the writing tasks at Key Stage 1. It is interesting in this context to note that at Herne Infants School, where the writing skills programme described above has been put into effect for several years now, the results for boys and girls on the writing task are very similar (as well as being considerably higher than average). This would seem to indicate that a carefully planned and structured programme of enjoyable activities can lead to very significant gains in writing achievement for boys, and can benefit girls too.

HIGH ABILITY AND HANDWRITING

There may also be specific reasons why highly able girls and boys find handwriting problematic in school. In the early stages of learning to write, it is likely to be a fairly slow and laborious task. Children need to focus on letter formation and pencil control, and the process is far from automatic at first. For some very able children, the discrepancy between the speed at which they are able to think and their writing ability causes significant frustration. This frustration is compounded by the fact that writing seems at the heart of school experience, and for some children can result in a negative attitude towards school. Some of these children already feel that they are failing in school at the tender age of five or six, which should never happen to any child.

There is also the issue of motivation, as for a bright child there can be enormous amounts of reward and satisfaction from other types of activity, such as designing or constructing a complicated machine, or reading a book, or using a computer programme to find out information. But for completing a page of writing, which may require much more effort, there is none – there may even be a disincentive in the form of a comment about how messy it is, or the child's own perception and dissatisfaction with the work. Children will not keep repeating an experience that is so demotivating, and may therefore develop a psychological block about writing, and be unwilling to produce more than a very small amount. This may in turn lead to a sense of failure in school, as writing appears to be such an important part of what happens there. If this continues for any length of time, there will be a serious impact on self-esteem.

Developing fluency in writing is an important goal (especially as external examinations still have a substantial requirement to write) but, as was seen earlier, there are more enjoyable ways to practise these skills than repetitive writing tasks, which many more able children will find difficult to tolerate. Children who feel in any way stressed and anxious about the process will not be able to perform to the best of their ability, not only because this impairs brain function, but because tension of any sort will be reflected in the muscles of the shoulders, arms and hands, thus inhibiting fluidity of movement in writing. It can be helpful to find alternative means of expression for children who have plenty to say but cannot yet write it down. Tape recordings, teacher (or classroom assistant) scribing, oral presentations and group work where only one or two children write things down can all be good methods of taking the pressure off for children who struggle with writing. Encouraging computer skills from an early age can also help, as children often enjoy playing with different fonts and colours for text. There are computer programmes (such as the currently available 'Clicker 5') which can provide 'scaffolding' so that very able children can write the stories that they can think. Many schools now use interactive whiteboards, and children enjoy writing on these with different colours and effects. Other schools have introduced different types and colours of pens in the early years for writing practice, which can add some interest (often a graphite pencil is a more difficult implement than a pen for achieving success in writing). For many children, a comfortable pen, a suitable angle to the page, and a sloping surface help to make the writing experience easier. Left-handed children are in particular need of this kind of support.

Writing tasks which encourage developing writers but are not too daunting include: labelling a diagram (particularly one of interest to the child, perhaps with some technical or unusual words); writing a note to someone with a particular purpose (to which it is important to get a written response); making a list (for birthday or Christmas, or for a picnic the class is planning, or some other real purpose). These tasks are similar to those where they may see adults use handwriting, and for more able children it is very important that they can see the purpose of using writing in a world where computers are used for most kinds of text.

LEARNING DIFFICULTIES AND HANDWRITING

It has already been noted in *Chapter 4* that some highly able children have a specific learning difficulty which may provide a barrier to effective learning in school. In particular, dyslexia and dyspraxia can both significantly affect handwriting ability. Montgomery (2003) gives practical advice for more able children with learning difficulties, and makes recommendations for interventions with dyslexic children which should be put in place from as early as possible, preferably as a child begins to learn to write. She emphasises the importance of joined letter patterns from the start, and testimony from some dyslexic adults confirms the added difficulty of having to learn to write twice, once printed and then 'joined up'. Joined letter patterns also help with spelling, as common patterns can be practised as a single movement.

It can be seen that the issue of handwriting is a complex one, and that there are differing reasons why highly able children may struggle with it. What is important, however, is the effect that this may have on their self-esteem. It is therefore vital in the early years of schooling to ensure that children have all the necessary support and help to do their best. We must not put obstacles in their way or focus unduly on areas of weakness at the expense of potential abilities and strengths.

CHAPTER 7

CHILDREN WITH SPECIAL ABILITIES IN LANGUAGE AND LITERACY

CASE STUDY

Deepak, 7

Seven-year-old Deepak was interested in language and symbols from a very early age, and by the age of eighteen months was memorising words in picture books, and was then able to transfer this knowledge to new books. His mother could not afford to buy books constantly, but such was Deepak's thirst for new reading material that they visited the library once or twice a week and always came back laden with as many books as they could borrow. His reading progressed rapidly, with encouragement from his parents but not a large investment of time (his new baby brother took up much of his mother's energy at this point, and she found it a relief that Deepak spent so much time reading quietly). One night when he was four years old she noticed his bedroom light on at midnight, and went to check up on him. He was wide awake in bed, eyes shining, having nearly finished reading *The Lion, The Witch and The Wardrobe*. The book had clearly excited him, so she had to let him finish the last few pages. She was extremely apprehensive about the start of school, but Deepak has been very lucky so far. He has had sympathetic teachers who have allowed him to read at his level, and sometimes gone out of their way to find interesting texts for him. They have given him challenges so that he doesn't always read the same kind of book.

For many highly able children and their parents, one of the first signs that the children may have special abilities is when they start to take an interest in letters and text of many kinds. They may start to recognise common signs seen frequently, such as the name of a supermarket or church. It is when they then remember the sign in a different context that some parents start to feel rather anxious, particularly if they are only around the age of two at the time. There is often a comparison with other children at nursery, playschool or toddler group, and it can be noticeable that in general the other children do not share this interest in books and the written word.

For other children the obsession can be with oral rather than written language, and so their speech develops faster and with more sophistication than that of other children (it may not start earlier − some parents report that the child said very little until able to talk in complete sentences). This development, as noted in an earlier chapter, can lead to problems with peers in early years settings, when a child expects that others will respond at the same level, and may well become frustrated when they can't.

Of course some children show advanced abilities in both reading and oral skills, and when these abilities are in step it is often easier to recognise them. Children who become absorbed in a book and do not say much, or children who always have much to say but find written texts more difficult to cope with, are more at risk of having their needs overlooked, both in supporting their considerable strengths and in devising appropriate ways to tackle their weaknesses. This chapter will attempt to address the different profiles of individual children who have special abilities in language and literacy, so not everything covered will be relevant for every child.

READING

There has been enormous debate for many years about the best way to teach reading and what system works most effectively. Highly able children who are naturally good at reading often seem to have learned in a fairly haphazard way, without much in the way of formal teaching, as they have been surrounded by text from the moment of birth. If they are fortunate, they have had chances to share books or other kinds of texts with adults or older siblings. Children who play computer games or watch advertisements on TV are bombarded with text and, just as the more musically able will pick up jingles and background music, so the more able in literacy will soon start to recognise words from their shapes.

More able readers often enjoy, and should be presented with, texts which contain challenges of various kinds. It is simply not necessary for a child who can already read to plough through a reading scheme in order to demonstrate this capability to another adult, and often this approach will do much to dishearten a child who previously enjoyed reading. Some children are happy to coast along at a level which is undemanding, and others simply ignore the school readers in favour of their own material, but little valuable learning is taking place.

It seems evident from looking at a wide variety of able children that they learn to read in different ways, and respond to different types of text. One five-year-old becomes fascinated by TV listings, while another is reading Roald Dahl. Both are using advanced literacy skills to decode what is of interest to them, but the outcome for them in a school setting might be very different, as the supply of suitable and motivating reading material for the former child within the classroom could be limited, and value judgements are often (sometimes subconsciously) placed on different kinds of texts.

Encouraging children to explore a wider variety of texts than the limits of their own instincts or knowledge is certainly a valuable part of education in literacy, but it is important to recognise the part played by motivation, and that however wonderful certain texts are considered to be by the teacher, there are those who will not easily engage with them. However, the teacher may succeed where parents do not, if sympathetic and 'tuned in' to a child. An example of this involved a six-year-old boy who loved all kinds of statistical information and fact books, but was not at all keen on reading fiction. As his older brother was a voracious reader of fiction there were many books available for the younger one to read, but he had not shown any inclination to do so despite encouragement from his mother. His reading skills were advanced for his age, and so the teacher brought to school a book she thought he would be able to read, more advanced than any of the Year 1 class readers. As he was very fond of this particular teacher and was obviously delighted that she thought he could tackle such a difficult book, he read it without complaint, and this was the start of a new adventure into fiction books of various kinds.

It is worth looking for very varied texts to have ready and available, as some are highly suited to encouraging bright readers out of their comfort zones. An example of this type of 'crossover' text is the 'Glory Gardens' series of cricket books by Bob Cattell, which contains very readable stories as well as match analysis and sporting comment, which will appeal to some. Roald Dahl's highly perceptive and subversive use of silliness and rudeness in adults (for example in *The Twits*, where the child can feel superior to the adult behaviour) has enticed many hitherto reluctant readers of fiction to see that story books can be fun. A similar awareness of five- and six-year-old children's preoccupations can be found in *The Giggler Treatment* by Roddy Doyle.

It is equally important to look for interesting ways to broaden the experience of those who only ever want to read fiction. Poetry in as many forms and shapes as possible can be inspiring, comforting or exciting for young children, and there has never been a greater range to choose from, whether old or new. The current Literacy Strategy rightly places value on many types of non-fiction text, and early readers now include fact books for children which are often more interesting than the somewhat limited stories.

SPEAKING

There is a resurgence of interest in encouraging young children to learn and practise speaking skills, as many teachers are aware that children who come into school now may be less developed in this area, if they live in a busy household with limited time for interaction, or where the television dominates other forms of communication.

There are, however, children who have special abilities in speaking as noted earlier, and these can cause difficulties for them if not handled carefully. A child with well-developed speech will be inclined to talk and chat at every available opportunity, and may find school rather daunting if the expectation is that children will sit and listen for any length of time, or work with limited talking. These children may not be advanced readers and writers (for many different reasons), so may not come to the attention of the teacher as having special abilities, but may instead be regarded rather negatively as they hold up the flow of the day with awkward questions or interesting observations. They may be inclined to try to monopolise the teacher's attention, as a conversation with classmates may not be so rewarding. Finding positive ways to cater for such children within a large class can be extremely difficult. But there is a serious risk that they will begin to lose interest in school, and feel that it doesn't provide for their needs, but only serves to highlight areas where they are not proficient.

Encouraging talk and discussion in problem-solving contexts can be done even with very young children, and is even more effective if specific training is given to the class, such as the 'Talk Lessons' proposed by Mercer (2000). If managed sympathetically it can be an important learning and growing experience for both the very talkative and dominant member of the class, and also for the quiet, shy one.

There is an increasing recognition that thinking skills are an important part of any curriculum, and that children's experiences of learning can be seriously enhanced by giving them opportunities to think and discuss. The growing 'Philosophy for Children' movement aims to encourage and facilitate these opportunities from a young age, and creative approaches to thinking such as 'thinking hats', thinkers' keys', 'thinking stories' and many others can help to create the community of enquiry that characterises a learning classroom (see Hymer and Michel, 2002, for a fuller discussion and inspiring examples of classes transformed in this way, as well as a useful resource list).

If due consideration is given to providing opportunities for meaningful and sustained discussion, and for sociable chatter as well, it should then be much more possible to help children realise that there are appropriate times for silence, for reflection and for listening. The creative use of music, art, stories and poetry will enhance these times in the classroom (or outside it).

WRITING

Some highly able children become prolific writers from an early age, spending hours of their spare time producing story after story. These young writers are easy to recognise, and can be valued and encouraged, but there are others whose abilities may well remain hidden, particularly if they experience early difficulty in handwriting (see *Chapter 6*). This highlights the importance of providing and encouraging alternative means of recording from an early age, so that the emergence of creative ideas and ways of thinking will not be missed or discouraged. This also makes writing into more of a 'real' task, as professional writers of all kinds use many different methods of recording their work.

There are many strategies for stimulating and encouraging children who show ability in writing of all kinds, and an excellent discussion of many of these can be found in Dean (2002). For younger children, Sutherland (2005) has some useful and varied suggestions.

It is crucially important that children are not put off writing as a result of their experiences in school. There has been considerable concern about the impact of National Curriculum testing on children's writing (see for example the website of the Literacy Trust for comments from QCA as well as from writers such as Michael Morpurgo and Philip Pullman). In particular, there is concern that the rather prescriptive way in which writing is sometimes taught (in order to maximise points within test marking schemes) can detract significantly from the idea of writing for sheer joy and pleasure. This may apply even more to older children, but the testing culture in which our schools and nurseries have to operate means that this sort of pressure sometimes begins from a very young age.

A research study in Kent looked specifically at the ways in which writing could be nurtured in young children. At first the emphasis was on boys, and specifically on using block play to facilitate narrative development. However, the study soon expanded to cover girls and boys in a variety of reception classes and nurseries. The resulting book 'Writing in the Air' (Marin 2003) documents the children's activities throughout the project. Teachers wrote down the children's stories as they told them when they were playing, and together with photos this resulted in books that the children wanted to hear and play again and again. Some children started to make books at home and parents were encouraged to become involved. For these children, writing (producing stories, letters, invitations and descriptions) was exciting and purposeful.

The following resources may be helpful for children with special abilities in language and literacy. They represent a small selection from the many which are available.

RESOURCES

www.teachernet.gov.uk/gtwise lists resources suitable for children with high abilities in many different subject areas including language and literacy. There is also an online forum where questions and messages can be posted.

www.nagcbritain.org.uk, the website of the National Association for Gifted Children, has an activities section for members (including school members) aged three to ten called Young Digitals. Activities are updated monthly and include language and literacy (this website is due for upgrading in 2007 and will offer some exciting new features).

www.bbc.co.uk/arts/books/ has a wealth of information, competitions and activities for readers and writers of all ages, with a section for Young Readers.

www2.sherston.com/freebees/literacy.htm contains free sample literacy activities suitable for early years and Key Stage 1.

www.literacytrust.org.uk contains reports and research on all aspects of literacy.

www.sebastianswan.org.uk encourages children to use ICT and contains online books and activities

Texts for further reading:

Dean,G. (2002) *Challenging the More Able Language User*. London: Fulton.

Fisher, R. and Williams, M. (2005) *Unlocking Literacy* (2nd ed). London: Fulton.

CHAPTER 8

MATHEMATICAL ABILITY

CASE STUDY

Andrew, 6

Andrew is a bright six-year-old boy, currently in Year 1, who has loved numbers and patterns since he was very small. He is constantly playing with numerical ideas in his head, and at five years old he invented a term for certain numbers, which he calls 'crinkly numbers'. These numbers have particular mathematical properties which he finds extremely satisfying. He is not really happy unless he is working on some form of mathematical problem, and finds many aspects of school very tedious indeed, especially the maths he is expected to do. He also finds it difficult to relate to his peers, as they do not find numbers fascinating in the way that he does.

A precocious mathematical ability in the early years at nursery and at school can cause many headaches for educators, who rightly see their role as providing enriched environments and opportunities for children to experience a broad and balanced range of activities. They may not understand that to a highly mathematical child, enjoyment and fulfilment come from playing with numbers and concepts, and that maths pervades every aspect of life. Some may feel slightly threatened or insecure, if their own experience of mathematics in school has been negative or they think they have never been good with numbers. It is difficult for them to grasp the idea that children can be passionate about something they perceive as hard work, or even to be feared. Reference to the various frameworks and criteria currently available for early years educators to teach mathematical concepts to young children certainly do not help, as for more able children they appear limiting and prescriptive. An example comes from the recent Foundation Stage Profiles, which provide steps for young children's attainment between the ages of three and five, up to the end of the reception year. One of the six areas of learning is Mathematical Development, and within this are several assessment scales, presented with eight steps, plus an extra one for exceptional performance. For the use and awareness of numbers for labels and counting, the exceptional performance at five years old is to use numbers up to 20. Many mathematically able children are counting to 20 at the age of two or three, and would feel thoroughly insulted if they were only expected to go as far as this at the age of five. The example of Andrew's crinkly numbers (which extended into the thousands) which he developed when he was five, and the story at the end of this chapter which was observed in a regular reception class in a mainstream school, show the futility of setting such arbitrary limits on children's learning. If enforced, mathematically able children will become frustrated, and this carries the significant risk that they will 'switch off' from the very subject in which they have the greatest potential. Repeated frustration could lead to a sense of alienation from school.

Many children, not just those with particular abilities, enjoy the concept of big numbers, and it can be exciting to talk about thousands, millions and billions. Though many children will not have a clear concept of (for example) a billion, it is doubtful whether many adults do either – the important point is to be thrilled by the idea.

This relates to another issue affecting mathematically able children – very often they do not learn in a linear fashion, but make conceptual leaps and jumps which can appear to be haphazard or uneven. Educators are often very worried about gaps in learning, and for many children this is a legitimate concern, but highly able children are usually able to fill the gaps in later on, maybe with a bit of help or scaffolding at the appropriate time. Insistence that children follow an imposed order or method can again stifle the enjoyment and fulfilment that they may feel from doing their own exploration.

As mentioned in *Chapter 4*, it is also important for children with special abilities to be working at a level where they will be making mistakes – not careless ones (often very bright children make silly slips if they find work too easy, as they don't take care). It is important that the work is challenging them in what Vygotsky called the Zone of Proximal Development (see *Chapter 2*) where they need some help to arrive at the right answer, which will then take them on to the next level of learning. This can be enormously difficult to provide for naturally mathematical children, but if they are allowed to coast along (and some will enjoy this as it leaves plenty of time for chatting or other distraction activities) then the time will come when, faced with a challenge, they do not know how to struggle to reach a solution.

Sometimes it is difficult to know how to handle a child who appears obsessed by numbers in the nursery, and reluctant to participate in other activities. It is important not to force cooperation, but it may be possible to entice the child if the activity is made tempting enough by relating it to mathematical concepts. For example, sand, water and even paint can be measured, toys can be sorted by colour, shape or size, many games and songs contain mathematical ideas, role play areas such as the shop or café lend themselves easily to mathematical activities, and stories can be woven around mathematical notions. This awareness of the maths that is all around us will benefit other children too in their mathematical development.

OBSERVATION – MONTESSORI NURSERY

An observer spent some time in the nursery with the children, and was particularly drawn to the maths area where there were many solid representations of mathematical concepts, all made from wood and beautifully coloured. It was possible to explore numbers up to a thousand, compare and sort by size, and experience a wide variety of solid shapes. At one point during the observation a little boy of four became extremely excited, jumping up and down clutching one of the solid shapes and exclaiming, 'It's an ellipsoid, it's an ellipsoid!' The observer had rarely seen such sheer joy in learning within an educational setting (see Counsell (2004a) for a full account of this observation).

The provision of such stimulating materials for children to explore would seem to be an important part of providing for the needs of mathematically able children. Koshy (2002) describes some items which might be found in a 'mathematics interest area', and goes on to give some useful ideas and suggestions for activities and strategies which will appeal to young children with special abilities in maths. There are many other sources of mathematical activities, some of which are included in the resource list at the end of this chapter, but this is by no means exhaustive.

It is important, too, to provide these opportunities without putting unnecessary obstacles in the way of children's efforts. Many young children with ability in mathematics are not particularly fond of writing, and endless sums which need to be written down will be extremely demotivating. Mathematical work can be done in many different ways – on the computer, with solid shapes and with other materials, and certainly does not always need to be recorded. Where written outcomes are required, these can be kept to a minimum for young children, as it is much more important that they enjoy their maths. For some highly able children, particularly after more formal learning is introduced in

Years 1 and 2, maths is a joyful subject as it does not require as much writing as other areas of the curriculum.

There are some wonderful examples of working with more able young children in maths from the local education authority of Medway, where the adviser for Gifted and Talented children has worked with G&T/More Able Coordinators within the borough to produce some guidelines for working with more able children in the early years. The resulting document, which is available from Medway council, is entitled *Guidance on Gifted and Talented (Very Able) Children in Foundation Stage*, and it is subtitled ∞ − 1 (infinity minus one). The subtitle itself relates to a mathematically able four year old, and her story is beautifully told in the booklet. Copies can be obtained from Krysia Baczala (krysia.baczala@medway.gov.uk). All the areas of experience in the Foundation Stage are covered in this booklet, not just mathematical ability.

RESOURCES

Some suggested resources follow for children with special abilities in mathematics. It is important to bear in mind that this is only a selection, there are many more resources and games available, including those in newspapers and magazines which can be collected and laminated to make more resources for mental starters, for example challenge boxes (see *Chapter 9*).

Let's Think Through Maths! Michael Shayer, Mundher Adhami and Anne Robertson. nferNelson. This is a pack of hands-on mathematical activities for 5–6 year olds, and includes a comprehensive teacher's guide.

Magimixer is a small device consisting of a frame with seven moveable dice, which can generate many sums and be used at different levels. Available from Hope Education (www.hope-education.co.uk).

There is also a card game called 24 from Summus UK (www.24game.com), in which you have to combine 4 numbers to make 24. This is available in various levels of difficulty.

www.nrich.maths.org contains many activities designed for children aged from four to nineteen who are more able in maths. There is a large archive of activities divided into topics, and new material is constantly being added. Some activities are suitable to do online, others for downloading and giving on paper.

www.worldclassarena.org is the website of the World Class Tests in mathematics and problem-solving for eight–eleven- and twelve–fourteen-year-olds. There is an online maths challenge which can be taken on the computer at any time, and will give feedback as to whether a child is a suitable candidate for the World Class Tests. The eight–eleven tests can be taken by children who are younger than this, if this is considered appropriate. QCA also produces supporting materials for teachers, which can be used in class.

www.teachernet.gov.uk/gtwise lists resources suitable for children with high abilities in many different subject areas including mathematics. There is also an online forum where questions and messages can be posted.

www.nagcbritain.org.uk, the website of the National Association for Gifted Children, has an activities section for members (including school members) aged three to ten called Young Digitals. Activities are updated monthly and include problem-solving and maths (this website is due for upgrading in 2007 and will offer some exciting new features).

The following books contain some mathematical activities which are suitable for younger children:

Koshy, V. and Casey, R. (1995) *Bright Challenge*, Stanley Thornes.

Teare, B. (1999) *Effective Resources for Able and Talented Children*,
   (2001) *More Effective Resources for Able and Talented Children*,
   (2003) *Challenging Resources for Able and Talented Children*.
   Network Educational Press.

In addition, the following texts have proved valuable to some young children with mathematical abilities:

Sachar, L. (1997) *Sideways Arithmetic from Wayside School*. US, Scholastic.

Norman, L.C. (1994) *Mathland – Novice Version*. Cambridge University Press.

Enzensberger, H.M.(1998) *The Number Devil – A Mathematical Adventure*. London, Granta.

CHAPTER 9

CLASSROOM STRATEGIES

ANIMAL SCHOOL – A FABLE

One day in Treetops Wood, it was decided by the animal council that a forest-wide curriculum should be established and made compulsory in all schools. Subjects to be covered were running, climbing, swimming and flying.

The animals in Class 1 at Bluebell School were very excited about starting school, and eager to learn new skills. Very soon, however, they began to experience problems in their classes.

The squirrel enjoyed the climbing classes, though he found them rather easy. His motivation and interest in school started to wane, however, when the teacher in flying class insisted he must start from the bottom and fly upwards, rather than from the top down.

The duck proved to be the best in the class at swimming, but found the running and climbing classes very difficult. As she had to keep repeating the exercises in these classes, her webbed feet became tired and worn, and her swimming suffered as a result. As she was still above average, the swimming teacher was not concerned.

The hare loved running, and easily won all the races. He became so despondent in flying class, however, that it affected all of his school experience and his parents decided to take him out of school.

The owl made an excellent start in flying class, but soon had an argument with her climbing teacher, as she had her own way of getting to the top of the tree which did not conform to the criteria for the subject laid down by the animal council.

In the end, the most successful student was a rather unusual eel who was good at swimming and could run, jump and fly a little.

(Author's adaptation - original source unknown)

This well-known fable illustrates a number of points about abilities, about differences, and about the nature and purpose of schools. I have heard many parents and children express the sentiment that school gets in the way of education, and it certainly seems that sometimes, sadly, this is so. How is it then possible to ensure that school or nursery provides something exciting and enriching for each child? And when focussing on the more able children, how can we give them a meaningful and positive experience, taking into account their individual differences and natural preferences?

Just as there is no such thing as a typical child with special abilities, so there is no one strategy or provision which will work well for all highly able children. This chapter covers approaches and issues which some schools have found helpful to consider in their efforts to meet the needs of more able children, and in many cases this has enriched the classroom experience of all the children, not just those with particular or recognised abilities.

DIFFERENTIATION

This term is often used to describe the way in which it is possible to meet the diverse learning needs which are found in every classroom. At the root of the word is the concept of difference – every child is different and provision needs to take account of this. As children with special abilities are very different from each other, the types of learning experience provided also need to vary.

Sometimes young children with abilities in particular areas will need something more complex to take account of these. An example might be in maths, where the class is looking at solid shapes. Some children may be fascinated by different shapes such as various types of prism. Young children need these shapes to be available to hold and feel, so it is important to have a wide range of solid shapes in the classroom. As well as liking to hold wooden shapes, many children will be fascinated by the effects of prisms and other solid shapes if they are made of glass or clear plastic, and these can feed the early interest in science that some young children clearly show. The important principle is not to limit opportunities for children, as far as this is possible.

At other times different learning experiences happen naturally from identical stimuli, and enriched provision with lots of different opportunities is sufficient to give all children access to challenge and growth. An example of this might be when a nursery teacher puts out 'small world' play figures with the building blocks to see what stories children can tell. The scope for firing children's imagination is increased, the resulting narratives will display many aspects of the children's creative abilities, but no two outcomes will be the same.

The American researchers Renzulli and Reis have written extensively about the need to 'compact the curriculum' for more able learners (Reis *et al*, 1994), and some schools have worked hard to adapt their principles to British schools. Central to this idea is an audit of what children already know, so that needless repetition can be avoided and children at all levels can make genuine progress. In the current educational climate there are signs that the DfES is taking the challenge of differentiation seriously in encouraging the development of 'Personalised Learning', which acknowledges that each learner is unique and approaches education in a different way.

ENCOURAGING THINKING SKILLS

In recent years there has been renewed interest in the development of children's thinking skills. A resurgence of interest in Bloom's taxonomy (*Figure 3*), classifying different levels of thinking, and identifying the higher-order thinking skills of analysis, synthesis and evaluation, has led to an increasing number of books and resources available to encourage these skills in the classroom, including some designed for use in the early years. A list of examples can be found at the end of this chapter.

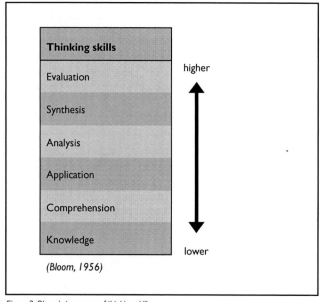

Figure 3: Bloom's taxonomy of thinking skills

The open-ended tasks designed to encourage and develop children's creative and critical thinking should ideally be used within a classroom environment where such thinking is encouraged as much as possible at all times. The day can start with a brainteaser or word puzzle already on display to tantalise the children as they arrive, and over time they can be encouraged to invent their own examples which can be shared with the class. 'Thought showering' activities can be used in many contexts, with the use of carefully designed open-ended questions linking to the topic under consideration (for example, a shared story, a maths activity or a discussion about culture or values). If children become accustomed to this type of thinking, their learning processes will become more efficient as they develop their metacognitive skills (thinking about how they think and learn). This approach often has a positive effect on group work, too, as children learn to value different contributions from varying perspectives. All children benefit from this, not just those with special abilities, though it will certainly appeal to them and give them scope to think at a challenging level.

More extended pieces of work which give plenty of scope for creative thinking will enable the further development and application of higher-order thinking skills. One example of such an activity is to design an underwater living centre (from Mowat, 2003). This activity starts with a thought-sharing exercise to see what the children think is needed to live successfully underwater. The children are then encouraged to sketch out their ideas, before finally drawing their centre on a large sheet of paper with coloured pens or pencils. This can be done collaboratively or individually, as an enrichment activity or as a whole class.

There are now many approaches available for helping all children to develop and use thinking skills. Many schools and classrooms have found the use of the 'Thinking Hats' (de Bono, 1999) a useful tool to encourage children's awareness of different kinds of thinking. TASC (Thinking Actively in a Social

Context) is another tool developed by Wallace (2000, 2002) which has been used successfully in many primary and early years classrooms. The 'Let's Think' materials (see *list of resources at end of chapter*) are designed for use with five to seven year olds across the ability spectrum. These were developed by Professors Adey and Shayer who helped to pioneer the CASE and CAME (Cognitive Acceleration in Science/Maths Education) approach which was shown to enhance effective thinking in older students through specific activities designed to promote thinking skills. Interestingly, improvements were seen not only in their maths and science lessons, but in other subjects too, showing that thinking skills once learned are highly transferable and can enhance all aspects of learning.

Philosophy for Children, often abbreviated to P4C, is an approach which builds on the use of thinking skills and metacognition to create a community of enquiry in the classroom. With young children the stimulus for philosophical thought is often a picture book, and some are particularly suitable for this purpose (see the list for example in Hymer and Michel, 2002). There are now many resources and ideas available to support the philosophical approach with young children, and educators have often been surprised at the way children (and not only those considered more able) have enjoyed and engaged with the opportunities to think and discuss on important issues.

ACCELERATION

There has been much debate about the best way to meet the needs of the more able pupil in a mixed class setting. Some experts are passionate advocates of one approach or another, sometimes recommending it across the board without regard for a particular child's profile and needs. It can be argued that a much more flexible approach is needed, looking at the individual child and the possibilities that exist within the setting. Acceleration is one commonly mentioned strategy for meeting the needs of the more able child, and encompasses several different practices, but they all share the idea of moving forward more quickly in the curriculum than is normally expected.

Complete acceleration is the moving of a child to a higher year group than the child's chronological age would dictate. This is sometimes called grade-skipping, and may involve a child missing a complete year of school (or more) or starting school at a younger age than normal. It is not a common practice in British state schools, and some Local Education Authorities have policies restricting the circumstances under which it can be done. In other LEAs it is left to the discretion of the headteacher.

Where this approach is used, it is often because it seems impossible to meet a child's advanced learning needs in the class corresponding to chronological age. Convenience for the teacher, however, is rarely a sufficient motive on its own to make the move desirable. There are many factors which must be taken into account, most importantly the social, emotional and physical maturity of the child. As school is primarily experienced as a social setting, these factors are enormously important to a child's self-esteem and confidence within it. The social effects of acceleration may not be seen until around the age of puberty, when increasing peer pressure and the drive to become more independent can prove problematic for a child who is younger than the others.

Many would argue, however, that it is simply not feasible to meet an exceptionally able child's learning needs in the class with chronological age peers, if there are no other children with similar ability in that class. A report on good practice in home-school relationships by the NAGC (Counsell, 2001) found several cases of children being accelerated in school, where parents and teachers alike had discussed and agreed that this was the best way forward, taking into account all the above factors. With the younger children in the study, it is not yet possible to say whether the strategy will work long-term, but for one of the older students it has indeed proved highly successful to the end of compulsory school age. It is interesting to note that in this case the acceleration was carried out more for social reasons than for academic ones, to provide a more suitable and sympathetic peer group for a highly able boy who had experienced considerable bullying and unhappiness at the start of secondary school.

With the existence of positive examples such as these, it is not possible to conclude that complete acceleration is never a wise option. Various research studies on grade-skipping in the US and Australia (for example Colangelo *et al*, 2004) seem to indicate many positive outcomes, but the school systems described are very different from British schools and it is not certain whether similar research here would produce comparable findings. Freeman (1998) laments the lack of information and research available on acceleration in the British context, which makes any judgement about the desirability or otherwise of accelerating more able children in school a difficult one, though her instinct is for caution.

There are several points which seem important in the consideration of whether complete acceleration (or early entry to school) will help a highly able young child. Assuming that social, emotional and physical maturity have been taken into account, it is also important to establish that once a child is in a class with older children, continuity of progression can be ensured. It would be extremely frustrating for a child to have to repeat a year later on in school, and this could more than undo any benefits of accelerating in the first place. While one or two families have come up with creative strategies to get round this (for example a gap year at age ten) this is certainly not feasible for most. Another important consideration is that the child is welcomed into the new class, and that the teacher is happy to have the child there. Acceleration by a year will not of itself meet a highly able child's learning needs, as in some areas children may be functioning two or three years (or more) in advance of chronological age, so differentiation will still be important. It should also be remembered, though, that skipping a year may mean that important information has been missed, so an opportunity to cover the key learning points needs to be provided. A highly able child is likely to be able to absorb these quickly and effectively, as long as they are suitably presented. A final consideration is that of handwriting which may not be as mature or well-developed as that of the other children, and allowances should be made for this, with alternative strategies provided at times (see *Chapter 6*).

Where complete acceleration is considered unwise or ruled out for other reasons, other types of acceleration are possible within a school or nursery context. Partial acceleration can mean that a child goes to another group or class for part of the time, maybe only for maths provision, or literacy. The bulk of the school day, including PE, assembly, art and craft activities and play times, is spent with the child's age peers. There can be advantages in this approach, as it can be used to recognise and provide for particular abilities, while at the same time acknowledging the importance of identifying with the peer group. However, there are again important factors which need to be considered for it to work successfully. Some children can become unsettled if they have to move to a different classroom for part of the day, and it can affect their sense of belonging to their class or group. Other children find a lack of maturity or less developed skills (such as writing) a problem in the new class setting. The teacher needs to be especially welcoming to the child, and it is important to find a 'buddy' within the new group. As partial acceleration can work well for some children, it can be tried out for a few weeks to assess whether it is a strategy that will help and support the child's learning needs.

EXTENSION AND ENRICHMENT

Another way to accelerate a child's learning is to provide materials designed for a higher age group. Although there is not complete agreement as to the exact meaning of this term, this is often referred to as extension, as the child's learning is being extended past the usual level for the age group. It happens in many classes quite naturally, as for example when more able readers go through the reading scheme more quickly and need books from the class above. This is usually fairly simple to track through the school, as the reading record of each child is individualised. It can be more tricky in other subjects such as maths or science, or the wider aspects of literacy, when individual work often follows on from whole class presentation, and is intended to build on it. A single child who is working a long way ahead may find the experience isolating, and whole class sessions pitched at a more basic level difficult to tolerate. Young children, especially, often find it hard to listen to and focus on something which does not engage them or present any kind of challenge. However, it is likely that these problems already exist for some more able children, so accelerated and extended work at certain times will still represent an improvement. It is obviously preferable if more than one child can work at a higher level, but this is not always possible.

Extension can also refer to tasks given which are not necessarily taken from higher year groups but which are more difficult and extend a child's thinking. Sometimes this is referred to as enrichment. For many children with special abilities, this type of task is important to keep them engaged and interested in their learning experience. It should not be offered simply as an add-on, but as an entitlement for the child who is capable of working at this level. The ideal task for a highly able child is at a level where there is an element of challenge which will need some adult help (in keeping with the concept of Zone of Proximal Development, see *Chapter 2*), but will lead to a great sense of satisfaction when accomplished. Of course, this is where all children should be working, but it can be more difficult to provide for a child who thinks and works at a higher level. Some of the resources listed at the end of this chapter are suitable for this kind of enrichment of the curriculum.

MENTORING

The concept of mentoring goes back to Greek mythology, where Mentor was the trusted friend and counsellor to Odysseus, and tutor to his son Telemachus. It is now widely used in education to refer to a number of similar practices, having in common the principle of support, which can be extremely beneficial to a child with special abilities (and to many other children). As with all provision, each child is different, so what suits one particular child may not be right for another.

There is a mentoring element to all early years teaching, as the teacher sets out to guide the young child into constructive learning experiences and, perhaps more than at any other stage of school education, tailors the provision to meet individual need. This personalised aspect can be developed further by providing more structured opportunities for a particular adult to work with one child in areas of special ability. This adult might be the class teacher (though time limitations could make this difficult), a classroom assistant, a volunteer parent, a school governor or other outside specialist or volunteer.

Another variation on the concept of mentoring has been the introduction in many schools of mini-mentoring schemes, which may also be called buddying or peer support. These can operate in various ways and for various purposes; they can be structured and a part of normal school routine or created especially as a one-off attempt to meet a particular need (see for example the case study of *Miriam* in *Chapter 4* who was paired with a Year 6 child who shared her interest in science). Where these schemes operate specifically for more able pupils, they often involve the pairing of a younger child with an older one, and this can have significant benefits for both parties. The older students gain from being in a responsible and supportive role, and if the pairing is managed carefully the younger children gains new friends, perhaps with shared interests or more able to meet the need to discuss topics at a higher level or in more depth.

CHALLENGE BOXES

A challenge box in the classroom can provide a useful strategy for times when it is impossible to provide extra teacher attention for pupils who have finished a task or need a challenge. The activities in a challenge box are designed to be fairly short (though they can sometimes lead to a more extended challenge if desired) and enjoyable. Examples might be brainteasers, comparisons (list all the ways a bird is similar to a helicopter), word puzzles and games (such as the popular Dingbats). These can be collected from many different sources, including newspapers, puzzle books and websites, and laminated to go in the box. Boxes can be swapped between classes for more variety. The idea can of course be adapted to suit different situations and particular topics, but the main principle is to increase motivation and provide a challenge.

SUGGESTED RESOURCES

This is a small sample of what is now available, chosen on the basis of ideas and activities suitable for younger children.

Thinking Out of the Box, **www.incentiveplus.co.uk**.
(200 thinking challenges, designed for a daily 'thinking slot')

Let's Think Through Science! Philip Adey, Frances Nagy, Anne Robertson, Natasha Street and Pam Wadsworth. nferNelson (designed to develop scientific thinking with 7–8 year olds)

Let's Think Through Maths! Michael Shayer, Mundher Adhami and Anne Robertson. nferNelson (hands-on mathematical activities for 5–6 year olds)

Teacher I've Finished Now What Do I Do? www.incentiveplus.co.uk (puzzles and thinking challenges for younger children)

Challenging Activities for Able and Talented Children Barry Teare, Network Educational Press
(contains a section for younger children)

Brilliant Activities for Gifted and Talented Children (That Other Children Will Love Too) Ashley McCabe Mowat. Brilliant Publications (brainteasers and longer activities to challenge thinking skills)

Gifted and Talented in the Early Years – Practical Activities for Children aged 3 to 5 Margaret Sutherland. Paul Chapman Publishing (activities and ideas in mathematics, language, music and physical movement)

http://puzzling.caret.cam.ac.uk
(science, arts and humanities puzzles aimed at older children but some would be enjoyed by younger ones with a particular interest)

www.nagcbritain.org.uk
(Young Digitals area contains puzzles for ages 3–10 accessible to members)

CHAPTER 10

WORKING WITH PARENTS

When children come into a nursery or school setting at the tender age of three or four, much of the process which makes them who they are has already taken place. Since they were tiny, helpless, newborn babies they have learned so many things – how to move and control their bodies, how to communicate with others, how to begin to interact with the world around them. Already their lives will have varied considerably – some will have grown up surrounded by toys, books and play equipment of all sorts. Others will not have had as much access to these things. For all children, their family and cultural experiences will have shaped their development and expectations. There is much research (see for example Schaffer, 1996) which suggests that the key factor in the child's developing self-esteem and ability to learn is the quality of the attachments formed with those who have cared for the child. There is also much research building on the theories of Vygotsky and Bruner (again see Schaffer) which shows that cognitive development in babies and young children takes place in social interaction and communication. Parents (here used to mean a child's main carers) are therefore hugely important in a child's education, and do not cease to be so once more formal education commences.

Like their children, parents come in all shapes and sizes. Some see themselves as an important part of the educational process, and have already spent considerable time with their children in planned educational pursuits (such as sharing books, music and gym classes, water and sand play, carefully graded toys). Others will be less confident about their role in education, maybe seeing this as something that happens at nursery or school. They may underestimate the amount that their children have already learned from them, and the value of one-to-one interactions with them in all kinds of spontaneous situations. If there is an extended family or several older siblings, a child may have grown up surrounded by chatter and talk, making a valuable contribution to development which is hard to measure. It is, however, important to recognise and value this in nursery or school, and to find a way to build on it, particularly if the language which has developed so richly does not happen to be English.

For some parents, however, school and education are rather alien territories not related to their everyday life. In families where there is trauma, poverty or struggle, where a parent feels isolated and unsupported, where children lack the daily comforts others take for granted, this can produce a situation which affects a child's development in a very negative way. Research carried out by organisations such as the DfES, Sure Start and the Literacy Trust (see *'useful websites'* section at the back of this book) shows how children's educational attainment is affected by poverty and deprivation. This highlights the importance of effective nursery provision for these children, which can provide for them some of the important interactions and stimulation they need to maximise their potential cognitively, emotionally, socially and physically. It is also important to find ways to involve and nurture parents so that they can be more effective in contributing to their children's development and education. Effective and positive action will raise the self-esteem of parents and children. Of course there are many circumstances in which this is extremely difficult, with numerous barriers to overcome, but unless parents are involved, the effectiveness of classroom interventions will be limited.

Schools have found many successful ways of involving parents with their children's education, such as bringing them into the classroom alongside their child, or setting up special groups for parents to learn more about the curriculum, or meeting places for parents in school to gather informally, perhaps with younger siblings. If parents are proving hard to engage, then some creative thinking needs to take place about how the school or nursery can take the initiative to involve them, and what sort of barriers may be encountered. The process will be different for every school, and for certain communities within schools, but it is a vitally important task which, if undertaken regularly and thoroughly, will enhance the learning and opportunities for children, and lessen the risk of underachievement.

In some schools, it may seem as if the opposite problem is faced. Highly articulate and possibly vociferous parents can be seen as extremely demanding, even pushy. Most teachers at some time have to deal with parents who are aggressive and make inappropriate demands. This can cause a natural wariness towards parents in general, which can be further exacerbated when dealing with parents who feel upset or angry, who may come across as hostile or defensive.

Many calls to the Helpline of the National Association for Gifted Children relate to concerns over whether and how children's needs are being met in school. Parents have sometimes had meetings with teachers but may feel that their concerns are not taken seriously, or they may not have even broached the subject of their dissatisfaction with the school for fear of being seen as 'pushy parents'. This can be even more relevant if parents feel that a child's high ability is linked to the problems in school. Yet if a child is not happy at school this can have a distressing effect on the whole family, so the sooner and more effectively things can be sorted out, the more positive the outcome is likely to be for everyone involved.

CASE STUDIES

Case studies describing some common causes for concern are outlined here, with questions for consideration, followed by some suggestions for strategies which may help schools and nurseries in their dealings with parents.

Asif, 4

Asif lives with his mother and two older sisters. From an early age his mother observed his interest in books and reading, and at the age of two he was looking at his older sisters' reading books and teaching himself to read. He would try to read everything – signs, posters and newspapers – and his mother looked forward to the start of nursery, as his incessant questions were very exhausting. However, he did not settle well in nursery, found peer relationships difficult and even started to get aggressive at times. The teachers were concerned about his behaviour, but Asif's mother feels that they did not recognise his advanced literacy or thirst for knowledge, which she feels contributed to the frustration he experienced in the nursery. At home he is lively and constantly 'on the go', but does not manifest the same type of aggressive behaviour.

Questions to consider:

1. What are some possible causes of Asif's behaviour?
2. Can you think of strategies which might help him?
3. What is the best way to work with Asif's mother?

Becca, 5

Becca has recently started school, and at home her favourite pastime is writing stories. She has a vivid imagination and is highly articulate for her age. However, at school she is very quiet and tends to copy what the others do. Her parents were distressed at a recent parents' evening that the teacher seemed to have no idea of Becca's capabilities.

Questions to consider

1. Why do you think Becca behaves this way in school?
2. What strategies might help her to demonstrate her ability?
3. What is the best way to work with Becca's parents?

Sam, 7

Sam's parents noticed from an early age that he liked to sing and make music, so they enrolled him in Kindermusik classes from the age of two. His teacher there was very impressed with him, felt he had musical talent and arranged for him to take violin lessons from the age of four. He has made significant progress on the violin and has now started piano lessons which he also enjoys. All his individual music teachers think he is very talented. His recent school report, however, in the 'Music' section, contains a brief comment that Sam joins in as required. Sam's father feels that his musical ability has not been recognised by the school, and he has consequently been overlooked for musical activities such as choir and recorder group.

Questions to consider:

1. How could this situation have been avoided?
2. What is the best way to work with Sam's father?

Anjuli, 7

Anjuli is an advanced reader and is also very good at maths. The school has acknowledged this and try to ensure that she is challenged appropriately in lessons. She is now a 'free reader', able to select her own reading books, and she is working on the top table in maths. Her parents feel that this is not enough and that she should be moved up a year. Her teacher and the headteacher feel that this is not a good idea, as Anjuli is already young in her year (her birthday is in June) and they are concerned for her emotional and social development, as well as the physical aspects (for example that she may be disadvantaged in PE).

Questions to consider:

1. How could you reassure Anjuli's parents that their concerns are being taken seriously?
2. Are there alternative strategies you could suggest which might be helpful for Anjuli?

It can be seen from these cases that communication between home and school is a key issue, of crucial importance if a child's needs are to be met effectively. Parents do not always supply information to the nursery or school about a child's abilities, often preferring teachers to recognise it for themselves. However, in a busy classroom, and with other factors such as a non-specialist teacher (particularly in areas such as music, art or PE) or a quiet child who does not want to do anything different from the others, abilities and potential can easily be overlooked, even within subject areas covered in school. How much more are abilities likely to be missed when they do not fall within the school curriculum as such (for example the little boy who built a washing machine from building blocks as described in *Chapter 4*)? A simple procedure to collect this sort of information routinely from parents would alleviate many of these problems and give class teachers useful information to build on with children, and ways to involve their interests and abilities in classroom activities. This could be done on admission, alongside information gathered about special needs and medical issues. Regular updates are needed as not all abilities will be apparent when starting school or nursery. Brief questionnaires before parents' evenings asking about particular concerns, needs or abilities would also be useful and would maximise the efficient use of the limited time available.

Some parents find meetings in school very stressful, and may find it very difficult to express their concerns for a variety of reasons. This may be because of their own negative experiences at school, or because they are emotional about the problems their child is experiencing. They may be worried about a potentially confrontational situation, or afraid to say what is making them anxious in case it sounds critical. They may feel intimidated because English is not their first language, and they find it hard to express what can be quite complex concerns. Careful, reflective listening is important in all these situations, making sure that underlying anxieties have been heard and that the discussion is not only focused on the teacher's priorities. Because teachers and educators are generally articulate, they can be very dominant in a discussion (not always intentionally) and if not careful can sound patronising or highly negative. As in all areas of school life, appropriate access to translated material or a translating service (whether professional or community-based) is vitally important so that all children can have their talents, abilities and potential recognised and valued.

When discussing a child's talents or gifts it is important to remember that ability is not something to be proved or disproved, but to be enhanced, nurtured and given the maximum opportunity to flourish. There is a common myth that all parents think they have gifted children, but parents usually know their children very well, they see them in a different context from school, one where children may be more relaxed, and so are often aware of abilities or potential that might be missed by the teacher.

It is also important to emphasise the common ground already shared by home and school. Both parents and teachers want children to be happy and achieve their best. They may differ in how best to achieve this, but if the aim is kept at the forefront of the discussion, this may help to defuse some of the tension and anxiety.

SOME KEY POINTS

- Include clear procedures for parent contact in all literature relating to admissions, school prospectus and regular newsletters.
- Collect routine information on children's abilities and update regularly.
- Ensure there is an area where parents can feel welcome and comfortable in school.
- If parents want to discuss concerns at a busy time, offer an appointment at a time which suits them.
- Reassure parents that their concerns are taken seriously and that the school will work with them to resolve any problems.
- Begin meetings with careful, reflective listening, encouraging parents to describe their concerns and checking to make sure you have understood.
- If concerns are raised at parents' evening, always offer a follow-up meeting to discuss in more detail.
- When a strategy is suggested or agreed, arrange a meeting within a suitable time so that feedback can be given from both sides.
- Find creative ways to involve parents in their children's education and in school life generally.

REFERENCES

Apple, M.W. and Teitelbaum, K. (2001) 'John Dewey' in Palmer, J.A. (ed), *Fifty Major Thinkers on Education*. London: Routledge.

Bergin, D.A. and Cizek, G.J. (2001) 'Alfred Binet' in Palmer, J.A. (ed), *Fifty Major Thinkers on Education*. London: Routledge.

Biddulph, S. (2003) *Raising Boys: Why Boys Are Different – and How to Help Them Become Happy and Well-balanced Men*. London: Thorsons.

Binet, A., Simon, T., (Reprint 1983) *The Development of Intelligence in Children*. Ayer Company, Salem, New Hampshire.

Browne, N. (1991) 'Girls' Stuff, Boys' Stuff': Young Children Talking and Playing. In Browne,N. (ed.) *Science and Technology in the Early Years: An Equal Opportunities Approach*. Buckingham: Open University Press.

Bruner, J. (1960) *The Process of Education*. Cambridge, MA: Harvard University Press.

Bruner, J. (1983) *Child's Talk: Learning to Use Language*. Oxford: Oxford University Press.

Colangelo, N., Assouline, S.G. and Gross, M.U.M., (2004) *A Nation Deceived: How Schools Hold Back America's Brightest Students*. University of Iowa.

Counsell, J. (2001) *Positive Home-School Liaison*. Milton Keynes: NAGC.

Counsell, J. (2004a) *Gifted and Talented Children in the Early Years*. Milton Keynes: NAGC.

Counsell, J. (2004b) *Highly Able Children and Handwriting*. Milton Keynes: NAGC.

Crocker, A. (2000) *Intelligence*. Milton Keynes: NAGC.

Davies, B. and Banks, C. (1992) The Gender Trap: A Feminist Poststructuralist Analysis of Primary School Children's Talk About Gender, *Journal of Curriculum Studies*, Vol. 24 (1). Basingstoke: Taylor and Francis.

De Bono, E. (1999) *Six Thinking Hats* (revised and updated version). USA: Little, Brown and Merry.

Dean, G. (2002) *Challenging the More Able Language User*. London: Fulton.

DfES (2004) *Key Stage National Summary Results*. www.standards.dfes.gov.uk

Dryden, G. and Vos, J. (1999) *The Learning Revolution*. USA: The Learning Web.

Eyre, D. (1997) *Able Children in Ordinary Schools*. London: Fulton.

Freeman, J. (1998) *Educating the Very Able: Current International Research*. London: The Stationery Office.

Freeman, J. (2000) Families: the Essential Context for Gifts and Talents. In Heller, K.A., Monks, F.J. and Passow, A.H. (eds.), *International Handbook of Research and Development of Giftedness and Talent*. Oxford: Pergamon Press.

Gardner, H. (1983) *Frames of Mind – the theory of multiple intelligences*. London: Heinemann.

Gardner, H. (2001) 'Jerome S. Bruner' in Palmer, J.A. (ed), *Fifty Modern Thinkers on Education*. London: Routledge.

Harrison, C. (2004), quoted on www.literacytrust.org.uk

Hartley-Brewer, E. (2000) *Raising Confident Girls – 100 Tips for Parents and Teachers*. London: Ebury Press.

Hymer, B. and Michel, D. (2002) *Gifted and Talented Learners – Creating a Policy for Inclusion*. London: Fulton.

Jacobs, J.E. and Weisz, V. (1994) Gender stereotypes: implications for gifted education. *Roeper Review*, Vol. 16.

Koshy, V (2002) *Teaching Gifted Children 4–7: A Guide for Teachers*. London, Fulton

Laevers, F. (1996) *The Leuven Involvement Scale for young Children (LBS-YC)*. Manual and Video-tape, Leuven: Centre for Experiential   Education.

Leyden, S. (2002) *Supporting the Child of Exceptional Ability at Home and   School*. London: Fulton

Marin, C. (2003) *Writing in the Air*. Kent County Council.

Mercer, N. (2000) *Words and Minds*. London: Routledge.

Montgomery, D. (2003) *Gifted and Talented Children with Special Educational Needs (Double Exceptionality)*. London: Fulton.

Mowat, A.M. (2003) *Brilliant Activities for Gifted and Talented Children (That Other Children Will Enjoy Too)*. Brilliant Publications.

Palmer, S. and Dolya, G. (2004) 'Freedom of Thought – a profile of Vygotsky' in *Times Educational Supplement*. July 30 2004.

Porter, L. (2001) *Gifted Young Children*. Buckingham: Open University Press.

Power, S., Whitty, G., Edwards, T. and Wigfall, V. (1998) 'Schoolboys and schoolwork: gender identification and academic achievement' in *ED826 Gender Issues in Education: Equality and Difference – Additional   Supplementary Readings*. The Open University.

Rauscher, F.H., Shaw, G.L. and Ky, K.N. (1993) Music and Spatial Task Performance. *Nature*, 365(6447): 611.

Reis, S. and Callahan, C.M. (1996) 'My Boyfriend, My Girlfriend, Or Me: The Dilemma of Talented Teenaged Girls', *Journal of Secondary Gifted Education*, Vol. 7(4).

Reis, S.M., Burns, D.E. and Renzulli, J.S. (1994) *Curriculum Compacting: The Complete Guide to Modifying the Regular Curriculum for High Ability Students*. Victoria: Hawker Brownlow Education.

Renzulli, J.S. (1986) 'The three-ring conception of giftedness: a developmental model for creative productivity' in Sternberg, R.J. and Davidson, J.E. (eds.) (1986) *Conceptions of Giftedness*. New York: Cambridge University Press.

Schaffer, H.R.(1996) *Social Development*. Oxford: Blackwell.

Schoenthaler, S. Amos, S., Eysenck, H., Peritz, E., and Yudkin,J. (1991) 'Controlled trial of vitamin-mineral supplementation: Effects on intelligence and performance,' *Personality and Individual Differences* 1991;12(4):343.

Smith, A. (1998), *Accelerated Learning in Practice*. Stafford, Network Educational Press.

Sternberg, R.J. (1997) 'A triarchic view of giftedness: theory and practice' in Colangelo, N. and Davis G.A. (eds.), *Handbook of Gifted Education*. 2nd Edition, Boston MA: Allyn & Bacon.

Sternberg, R.J. and Davidson, J.E. (eds) (1986) *Conceptions of Giftedness*. New York: Cambridge University Press.

Stopper, M. (ed) (2000) *Meeting the Social and Emotional Needs of Gifted and Talented Children*. London: Fulton.

Sutherland, M. (2005) *Gifted and Talented in the Early Years*. London, Paul Chapman Publishing.

Taylor, S. (2001) *Gifted and Talented Children – A Planning Guide.* London: Jessica Kingsley.

Thomas, F. (1997) *Une Question de Writing.* Teacher Training Agency/ Herne Infant School.

Wallace, B. (2000) *Teaching the Very Able Child – Developing a Policy and Adopting Strategies for Provision.* London: Fulton.

Wallace, B. (2002) *Teaching Thinking Skills Across the Early Years.* London: Fulton.

Walsh, D.J., Chung, S. and Tufekci, A. (2001) 'Friedrich Wilhelm Froebel' in Palmer, J.A. (ed), *Fifty Major Thinkers on Education.* London: Routledge.

Wood, D.J., Bruner, J.S. and Ross, G. (1976) 'The role of tutoring in problem solving', *Journal of Child Psychology and Psychiatry* 17: 89–100.

USEFUL WEBSITES

This is a general list of websites with useful information for teachers and parents about special abilities and issues raised in this book. Sites where there is specific advice and information relevant to children in the early years have been marked with *. All websites were accessible in January 2007.

www.standards.dfes.gov.uk/giftedandtalented The DfES website with news and information.

www.teachernet.gov.uk/gtwise A portal site with links, information and reviews of resources.

www.nc.uk.net/gt National Curriculum subject specific guidance with case studies.

www.nagcbritain.org.uk* The website of the National Association for Gifted Children, who support families of children with high abilities and provide information, links and activities for members.

www.nace.co.uk The website of the National Association for Able Children in Education who provide resources, support and training for teachers.

www.nagty.ac.uk The website of the National Academy for Gifted and Talented Youth, who are starting to offer some primary programmes.

www.talentladder.org.uk Guidance in identification and provision for high abilities in sport.

www.creativegeneration.org.uk Guidance in identification and provision for high abilities in art and design, dance, drama and music.

www.literacytrust.org.uk* Reports and research on all aspects of literacy.